THE ART
OF WAR

THE ART OF WAR

SUN TZŬ

Foreword by JAMES CLAVELL

HODDER
MOBIUS

Foreword by James Clavell © 1981 James Clavell

First published in Great Britain in 1981 by Hodder and Stoughton
A division of Hodder Headline

This revised edition published in 2005

A Mobius book

7

A CIP catalogue record for this title is
available from the British Library

ISBN 978 0 340 27604 4

Typeset in Monotype Sabon by Palimpsest Book Production Limited,
Polmont, Stirlingshire
Printed and bound in Great Britain by Clays Ltd, Elcograf S.p.A.

Hodder Headline's policy is to use papers that are natural,
renewable and recyclable products and made from wood grown in
sustainable forests. The logging and manufacturing processes are expected
to conform to the environmental regulations of the country of origin

Hodder and Stoughton Ltd
A division of Hodder Headline
338 Euston Road
London NW1 3BH

Contents

Foreword

Sun Tzŭ wrote this extraordinary book in China two and a half thousand years ago. It begins:

> The art of war is of vital importance to the state. It is a matter of life and death. A road to either safety or to ruin. Hence it is a subject of enquiry which can on no account be neglected.' It ends: 'Hence it is only the enlightened ruler and the wise general who will use the highest intelligence of the army for purposes of spying, and thereby they achieve great results. Spies are a most important element in war because upon them depends an army's ability to move.

I truly believe that if our military and political leaders in recent times had studied this work of genius, Vietnam could not have happened as it happened; we would not have lost the war in Korea (we lost because we did not achieve victory); the Bay of Pigs could not have occurred; the hostage fiasco in Iran would not have come to pass; the British Empire would not have been dismembered; and, in all probability, World Wars I and II would have been avoided – certainly they would not have been waged as they were waged, and the millions of youths obliterated unnecessarily and stupidly by monsters calling themselves generals would have lived out their lives according to their own Karma.

> 'The supreme act of war is to subdue the enemy *without fighting* . . .'

I find it astounding that Sun Tzŭ wrote so many truths twenty-five centuries ago that are so applicable today. I think this little book shows so clearly what is still being done wrong, and why our present opponent is so successful in some areas (Sun Tzŭ is obligatory reading in the Soviet political-military hierarchy and has been available in Russian for centuries. It is the source of all Mao Tse-tung's strategic and tactical doctrine).

Even more importantly, I believe the Art of War shows quite clearly *how to take the initiative* and combat the enemy – any enemy.

> 'Know your enemy, know yourself and you can fight a hundred
> battles without disaster . . .'

The first time I ever personally heard about Sun Tzŭ was at the races in Happy Valley in Hong Kong in 1977. A friend, P. G. Williams, a Steward of the Jockey Club, asked me if I had ever read the book. When I said no, he told me that he would be happy to send me a copy the next day. When the book arrived, I left it unread. Then one day, weeks later, I picked it up. I was totally shocked that, in all of my reading about Asia, about Japan and China particularly, I had not come across this book before. Since that time it has been a constant companion for me, so much so that during the course of the writing of *Noble House* many of the characters in it refer to Sun Tzŭ in all his glory.

Unfortunately little is known of the man himself. He wrote the thirteen chapters in approximately 490 BC in the Kingdom of Wu. About 100 BC one of his chroniclers, Su-ma Ch'ien, gives this biography:

> Sun Tzŭ whose personal name was Wu was a native of the
> Ch'i State. His Art of War brought him to the notice of Ho
> Lu, King of Wu. Ho Lu said to him, 'I have carefully perused
> your thirteen chapters. May I submit your theory of managing
> soldiers to a slight test.'
>   Sun Tzŭ replied, 'You may.'

The King asked, 'May the test be applied to women?'

The answer was again in the affirmative, so arrangements were made to bring 180 ladies out of the palace. Sun Tzŭ divided them into two companies and placed one of the King's favourite concubines at the head of each. He then made them all take spears in their hands and addressed them thus: 'I presume you know the difference between front and back, right hand and left hand?'

The girls replied, 'Yes.'

Sun Tzŭ went on. 'When I say eyes front, you must look straight ahead. When I say "left turn", you must face towards your left hand. When I say "right turn", you must face towards your right hand. When I say "about turn", you must face right around towards the back.'

Again the girls assented. The words of command having been thus explained, he set up the halberds and battle axes in order to begin the drill. Then to the sound of drums he gave the order 'right turn', but the girls only burst out laughing.

Sun Tzŭ said patiently, 'If words of command are not clear and distinct, if orders are not thoroughly understood, then the general is to blame.' He started drilling them again and this time gave the order 'left turn', whereupon the girls once more burst into fits of laughter.

Then he said, 'If words of command are not clear and distinct, if orders are not thoroughly understood, the general is to blame. But, if his orders are *clear* and the soldiers nevertheless disobey, then it is the fault of their officers.' So saying, he ordered the leaders of the two companies to be beheaded. Now the King of Wu was watching from the top of a raised pavilion, and when he saw that his favourite concubines were about to be executed, he was greatly alarmed and hurriedly sent down the following message: 'We are now quite satisfied as to our general's ability to handle troops. If we are bereft of these two concubines, our meat and drink will lose their savour. It is our wish that they shall not be beheaded.'

3

Sun Tzŭ replied even more patiently: 'Having once received His Majesty's commission to be general of his forces, there are certain commands of His Majesty which, acting in that capacity, I am unable to accept.' Accordingly, and immediately, he had the two leaders beheaded and straight away installed the pair next in order as leaders in their place. When this had been done the drum was sounded for the drill once more. The girls went through all the evolutions, turning to the right or to the left, marching ahead or wheeling about, kneeling or standing, with perfect accuracy and precision, not venturing to utter a sound.

Then Sun Tzŭ sent a messenger to the King saying: 'Your soldiers, Sire, are now properly drilled and disciplined and ready for Your Majesty's inspection. They can be put to any use that their sovereign may desire. Bid them go through fire and water and they will not now disobey.'

But the King replied: 'Let our general cease drilling and return to camp. As for us, we have no wish to come down and inspect the troops.'

Thereupon Sun Tzŭ said calmly: 'The King is only fond of words and cannot translate them into deeds.'

After that the King of Wu saw that Sun Tzŭ was one who knew how to handle an army, and appointed him general. In the West Sun Tzŭ defeated the Ch'u State and forced his way into Ying, the capital; to the North he put fear into the States of Ch'i and Chin, and spread his fame abroad amongst the feudal princes. And Sun Tzŭ shared in the might of the Kingdom.

Sun Tzŭ became a general for the King of Wu in 512 BC. For almost two decades the armies of Wu were victorious over their hereditary enemies, the Kingdom of Yueh and Ch'u. Some time within this period Sun Tzŭ died. His patron, Ho Lu, King of Wu, was killed in a battle in 496 BC. For a few years his descendants followed the precepts of Sun Tzŭ and continued to be victorious. And then they forgot. In 473 BC the armies of Wu were defeated and the Kingdom made extinct.

In 1782 *The Art of War* was first translated into French by a Jesuit, Father Amiot. There is a legend that this little book was Napoleon's key to success and his secret weapon. Certainly his battles depended upon mobility, and mobility is one of the things that Sun Tzŭ stresses. Certainly Napoleon used all of Sun Tzŭ to his own advantage to conquer most of Europe. It was only when he failed to follow Sun Tzŭ's rules that he was defeated.

The Art of War was not translated into English until 1905. The first English translation was by P. F. Calthrop. The second, the one that you will read here, is by Lionel Giles, originally published in Shanghai and London in 1910. I have edited it here and there to make it a little more simple, but I have left his translation intact and also his notes – the notes inserted according to the Chinese method, immediately after the passages to which they refer.

I sincerely hope you enjoy reading this book. Certainly I would like to make it obligatory study for all our serving officers and men, all politicians and all people in government and universities in the free world. If I was a commander-in-chief or President or Prime Minister I would go further: I would have written into law that all officers, *particularly all generals*, take a yearly oral and written examination on these 13 chapters, the pass mark being 95 per cent – any general failing to achieve a pass to be automatically and summarily fired without appeal, and all other officers to have automatic demotion.

I believe, very much, Sun Tzŭ's knowledge is vital to our survival. It can give us the protection we need to watch our children grow in peace, and thrive peacefully . . . '*The purpose of war is peace.*'

'In peace prepare for war, in war prepare for peace. The art of war is of vital importance to the state. It is a matter of life and death. A road either to safety or ruin. Hence it is a subject of enquiry which *can on no account be neglected . . .*'

JAMES CLAVELL
Lookout Mountain, California.
May, 1981

THE BOOK

I Laying Plans

1. Sun Tzŭ said: The art of war is of vital importance to the State.

2. It is a matter of life and death, a road either to safety or to ruin. Hence it is a subject of inquiry which can on no account be neglected.

3. The art of war, then, is governed by five constant factors, to be taken into account in one's deliberations, when seeking to determine the conditions obtaining in the field.

4. These are: (1) The Moral Law; (2) Heaven; (3) Earth; (4) The Commander; (5) Method and discipline.

5, 6. *The Moral Law* causes the people to be in complete accord with their ruler, so that they will follow him regardless of their lives, undismayed by any danger.

7. *Heaven* signifies night and day, cold and heat, times and seasons.

8. *Earth* comprises distances, great and small; danger and security; open ground and narrow passes; the chances of life and death.

9. *The Commander* stands for the virtues of wisdom, sincerity, benevolence, courage and strictness.

The five cardinal virtues of the Chinese are (1) humanity or benevolence; (2) uprightness of mind; (3) self-respect, self-control, or 'proper feeling'; (4) wisdom; (5) sincerity or good faith.

10. By *Method and discipline* are to be understood the marshalling of the army in its proper subdivisions, the gradations of rank among the officers, the maintenance of roads by which supplies may reach the army, and the control of military expenditure.

11. These five heads should be familiar to every general: he who knows them will be victorious; he who knows them not will fail.

12. Therefore, in your deliberations, when seeking to determine the military conditions, let them be made the basis of a comparison, in this wise.

13. (1) Which of the two sovereigns is imbued with the Moral law?

(2) Which of the two generals has most ability?

(3) With whom lie the advantages derived from Heaven and Earth?

(4) On which side is discipline most rigorously enforced?

Tu Mu alludes to the remarkable story of Ts'ao Ts'ao (A.D. 155–220), who was such a strict disciplinarian that once, in accordance with his own severe regulations against injury to standing crops, he condemned himself to death for having allowed his horse to shy into a field of corn! However, in lieu of losing his head, he was persuaded to satisfy his sense of justice by cutting off his hair. 'When you lay down a law, see that it is not disobeyed; if it is disobeyed, the offender must be put to death.'

(5) Which army is the stronger?

(6) On which side are officers and men more highly trained?

'Without constant practice, the officers will be nervous and undecided when mustering for battle; without constant practice, the general will be wavering and irresolute when the crisis is at hand.'

(7) In which army is there the greater constancy both in reward and punishment?

That is, on which side is there the most absolute certainty that merit will be properly rewarded and misdeeds summarily punished?

14. By means of these seven considerations I can forecast victory or defeat.

15. The general that hearkens to my counsel and acts upon it, will conquer – let such a one be retained in command! The general that hearkens not to my counsel nor acts upon it, will suffer defeat – let such a one be dismissed!

16. While heeding the profit of my counsel, avail yourself also of any helpful circumstances over and beyond the ordinary rules.

17. According as circumstances are favourable, one should modify one's plans.

Sun Tzŭ, as a practical soldier, cautions us here not to pin our faith to abstract principles; 'for,' as Chang Yü puts it, 'while the main laws of strategy can be stated clearly enough for the benefit of all and sundry, you must be guided by the actions of the enemy in attempting to secure a favourable position in actual warfare.' On the eve of the battle of Waterloo, Lord Uxbridge, commanding the cavalry, went to the Duke of Wellington in order to learn what his plans and calculations were for the morrow, because, as he explained, he might suddenly find himself Commander-in-chief and would be unable to frame new plans in a critical moment. The Duke listened quietly and then said: 'Who will attack the first to-morrow – I or Bonaparte?' 'Bonaparte,' replied Lord Uxbridge. 'Well,' continued the Duke, 'Bonaparte has not given me any idea of his projects; and as my plans will depend upon his, how can you expect me to tell you what mine are?'

18. All warfare is based on deception.

The truth of this pithy and profound saying will be admitted by every soldier. Wellington, great in so many military qualities, was especially distinguished by 'the extraordinary skill with which he concealed his movements and deceived both friend and foe.'

19. Hence, when able to attack, we must seem unable; when using our forces, we must seem inactive; when we are near, we must make the enemy believe we are far away; when far away, we must make him believe we are near.

20. Hold out baits to entice the enemy. Feign disorder, and crush him.

21. If he is secure at all points, be prepared for him. If he is in superior strength, evade him.

22. If your opponent is of choleric temper, seek to irritate him. Pretend to be weak, that he may grow arrogant.

The good tactician plays with his adversary as a cat plays with a mouse, first feigning weakness and immobility, and then suddenly pouncing upon him.

23. If he is taking his ease, give him no rest. If his forces are united, separate them.

24. Attack him where he is unprepared, appear where you are not expected.

25. These military devices, leading to victory, must not be divulged beforehand.

26. Now the general who wins a battle makes many calculations in his temple ere the battle is fought. The general who

loses a battle makes but few calculations beforehand. Thus do many calculations lead to victory, and few calculations to defeat: how much more no calculation at all! It is by attention to this point that I can foresee who is likely to win or lose.

II Waging War

'He who wishes to fight must first count the cost,' which prepares us for the discovery that the subject of the chapter is not what we might expect from the title, but is primarily a consideration of ways and means.

1. Sun Tzŭ said: In the operations of war, where there are in the field a thousand swift chariots, as many heavy chariots, and a hundred thousand mail-clad soldiers, with provisions enough to carry them a thousand *li*,* the expenditure at home and at the front, including entertainment of guests, small items such as glue and paint, and sums spent on chariots and armour, will reach the total of a thousand ounces of silver per day. Such is the cost of raising an army of 100,000 men.

2. When you engage in actual fighting, if victory is long in coming, the men's weapons will grow dull and their ardour will be damped. If you lay siege to a town, you will exhaust your strength.

3. Again, if the campaign is protracted, the resources of the State will not be equal to the strain.

4. Now, when your weapons are dulled, your ardour damped, your strength exhausted and your treasure spent, other chieftains will spring up to take advantage of your extremity. Then no man, however wise, will be able to avert the consequences that must ensue.

---

* 2.78 modern *li* go to a mile. The length may have varied slightly since Sun Tzŭ's time.

5. Thus, though we have heard of stupid haste in war, cleverness has never been seen associated with long delays.

6. There is no instance of a country having benefited from prolonged warfare.

7. It is only one who is thoroughly acquainted with the evils of war that can thoroughly understand the profitable way of carrying it on.

That is, with rapidity. Only one who knows the disastrous effects of a long war can realise the supreme importance of rapidity in bringing it to a close.

8. The skilful soldier does not raise a second levy, neither are his supply-waggons loaded more than twice.

Once war is declared, he will not waste precious time in waiting for reinforcements, nor will he turn his army back for fresh supplies, but crosses the enemy's frontier without delay. This may seem an audacious policy to recommend, but with all great strategists, from Julius Caesar to Napoleon Bonaparte, the value of time – that is, being a little ahead of your opponent – has counted for more than either numerical superiority or the nicest calculations with regard to commissariat.

9. Bring war material with you from home, but forage on the enemy. Thus the army will have food enough for its needs.

10. Poverty of the State exchequer causes an army to be maintained by contributions from a distance. Contributing to maintain an army at a distance causes the people to be impoverished.

11. On the other hand, the proximity of an army causes prices to go up; and high prices cause the people's substance to be drained away.

12. When their substance is drained away, the peasantry will be afflicted by heavy exactions.

13, 14. With this loss of substance and exhaustion of strength, the homes of the people will be stripped bare, and three-tenths of their incomes will be dissipated; while Government expenses for broken chariots, worn-out horses, breast-plates and helmets, bows and arrows, spears and shields, protective mantlets, draught-oxen and heavy waggons, will amount to four-tenths of its total revenue.

> 'The *people* being regarded as the essential part of the State, and *food* as the people's heaven, is it not right that those in authority should value and be careful of both?'

15. Hence a wise general makes a point of foraging on the enemy. One cartload of the enemy's provisions is equivalent to twenty of one's own, and likewise a single picul of his provender is equivalent to twenty from one's own store.

> Because twenty cartloads will be consumed in the process of transporting one cartload to the front.

16. Now in order to kill the enemy, our men must be roused to anger; that there may be advantage from defeating the enemy, they must have their rewards.

> 'Rewards are necessary in order to make the soldiers see the advantage of beating the enemy; thus, when you capture spoils from the enemy, they must be used as rewards, so that all your men may have a keen desire to fight, each on his own account.'

17. Therefore in chariot fighting, when ten or more chariots have been taken, those should be rewarded who took the first. Our own flags should be substituted for those of the enemy, and the chariots mingled and used in conjunction with ours. The captured soldiers should be kindly treated and kept.

18. This is called, using the conquered foe to augment one's own strength.

19. In war, then, let your great object be victory, not lengthy campaigns.

'War is not a thing to be trifled with.'

20. Thus it may be known that the leader of armies is the arbiter of the people's fate, the man on whom it depends whether the nation shall be in peace or in peril.

III Attack by Stratagem

1. Sun Tzŭ said: In the practical art of war, the best thing of all is to take the enemy's country whole and intact; to shatter and destroy it is not so good. So, too, it is better to capture an army entire than to destroy it, to capture a regiment, a detachment or a company entire than to destroy them.

2. Hence to fight and conquer in all your battles is not supreme excellence; supreme excellence consists in breaking the enemy's resistance without fighting.

3. Thus the highest form of generalship is to baulk the enemy's plans; the next best is to prevent the junction of the enemy's forces;

> Isolating him from his allies. We must not forget that Sun Tzŭ, in speaking of hostilities, always has in mind the numerous states or principalities into which the China of his day was split up.

the next in order is to attack the enemy's army in the field;

> When he is already in full strength.

and the worst policy of all is to besiege walled cities.

4. The rule is, not to besiege walled cities if it can possibly be avoided.

The preparation of mantlets, movable shelters, and various implements of war, will take up three whole months; and the piling up of mounds over against the walls will take three months more.

5. The general, unable to control his irritation, will launch his men to the assault like swarming ants, with the result that one-third of his men are slain, while the town still remains untaken. Such are the disastrous effects of a siege.

6. Therefore the skilful leader subdues the enemy's troops without any fighting; he captures their cities without laying siege to them; he overthrows their kingdom without lengthy operations in the field.

7. With his forces intact he will dispute the mastery of the Empire, and thus, without losing a man, his triumph will be complete.

This is the method of attacking by stratagem.

8. It is the rule in war, if our forces are ten to the enemy's one, to surround him; if five to one, to attack him; if twice as numerous, to divide our army into two.

'If our force is twice as numerous as that of the enemy, it should be split up into two divisions, one to meet the enemy in front, and one to fall upon his rear; if he replies to the frontal attack, he may be crushed from behind; if to the rear-ward attack, he may be crushed in front. This is what is meant by saying that "one part may be used in the regular way, and the other for some special diversion."'

9. If equally matched, we can offer battle;

'If attackers and attacked are equally matched in strength, only the able general will fight.'

if slightly inferior in numbers, we can avoid the enemy; if quite unequal in every way, we can flee from him.

10. Hence, though an obstinate fight may be made by a small force, in the end it must be captured by the larger force.

11. Now the general is the bulwark of the State: if the bulwark

is complete at all points, the State will be strong; if the bulwark is defective, the State will be weak.

12. There are three ways in which a ruler can bring misfortune upon his army:

13. (1) By commanding the army to advance or to retreat, being ignorant of the fact that it cannot obey. This is called hobbling the army.

> 'A kingdom should not be governed from without, an army should not be directed from within.' Of course it is true that, during an engagement, or when in close touch with the enemy, the general should not be in the thick of his own troops, but a little distance apart. Otherwise, he will be liable to misjudge the position as a whole, and give wrong orders.

14. (2) By attempting to govern an army in the same way as he administers a kingdom, being ignorant of the conditions which obtain in an army. This causes restlessness in the soldiers' minds.

> 'The military sphere and the civil sphere are wholly distinct; you can't handle an army in kid gloves.' And: 'Humanity and justice are the principles on which to govern a state, but not an army; opportunism and flexibility, on the other hand, are military rather than civic virtues.'

15. (3) By employing the officers of his army without discrimination,

> That is, he is not careful to use the right man in the right place.

through ignorance of the military principle of adaptation to circumstances. This shakes the confidence of the soldiers.

> 'If a general is ignorant of the principle of adaptability, he must not be entrusted with a position of authority.' The skilful employer of men will employ the wise man, the brave man,

the covetous man, and the stupid man. For the wise man delights in establishing his merit, the brave man likes to show his courage in action, the covetous man is quick at seizing advantages, and the stupid man has no fear of death.'

16. But when the army is restless and distrustful, trouble is sure to come from the other feudal princes. This is simply bringing anarchy into the army, and flinging victory away.

17. Thus we may know that there are five essentials for victory:
    (1) He will win who knows when to fight and when not to fight.

'If he can fight, he advances and takes the offensive; if he cannot fight, he retreats and remains on the defensive. He will invariably conquer who knows whether it is right to take the offensive or the defensive.'

(2) He will win who knows how to handle both superior and inferior forces.

This is not merely the general's ability to estimate numbers correctly: 'By applying the art of war, it is possible with a lesser force to defeat a greater, and *vice versa*. The secret lies in an eye for locality, and in not letting the right moment slip. With a superior force, make for easy ground; with an inferior one, make for difficult ground.'

(3) He will win whose army is animated by the same spirit throughout all its ranks.
(4) He will win who, prepared himself, waits to take the enemy unprepared.
(5) He will win who has military capacity and is not inter-fered with by the sovereign.

'It is the sovereign's function to give broad instructions, but to decide on battle is the function of the general.' It is needles to dilate on the military disasters which have been caused by undue interference with operations in the field on the part of the home government. Napoleon undoubtedly owed much of his extraordinary success to the fact that he was not hampered by any central authority.

Victory lies in the knowledge of these five points.

18. Hence the saying: If you know the enemy and know yourself, you need not fear the result of a hundred battles. If you know yourself but not the enemy, for every victory gained you will also suffer a defeat. If you know neither the enemy nor yourself, you will succumb in every battle.

'Knowing the enemy enables you to take the offensive, knowing yourself enables you to stand on the defensive. Attack is the secret of defence; defence is the planning of an attack.'

IV Tactical Dispositions

1. Sun Tzŭ said: The good fighters of old first put themselves beyond the possibility of defeat, and then waited for an opportunity of defeating the enemy.

2. To secure ourselves against defeat lies in our own hands, but the opportunity of defeating the enemy is provided by the enemy himself.

3. Thus the good fighter is able to secure himself against defeat,

'By concealing the disposition of his troops, covering up his tracks, and taking unremitting precautions' (Chang Yü).

but cannot make certain of defeating the enemy.

4. Hence the saying: One may *know* how to conquer without being able to *do* it.

5. Security against defeat implies defensive tactics; ability to defeat the enemy means taking the offensive.

6. Standing on the defensive indicates insufficient strength: attacking, a superabundance of strength.

7. The general who is skilled in defence hides in the most secret recesses of the earth; he who is skilled in attack flashes forth from the topmost heights of heaven. Thus on the one hand we have ability to protect ourselves; on the other, a victory that is complete.

8. To see victory only when it is within the ken of the common herd is not the acme of excellence.

9. Neither is it the acme of excellence if you fight and conquer and the whole Empire says, 'Well done!'

True excellence being, 'To plan secretly, to move surreptitiously, to foil the enemy's intentions and baulk his schemes, so that at last the day may be won without shedding a drop of blood.'

10. To lift an autumn hair is no sign of great strength; to see sun and moon is no sign of sharp sight; to hear the noise of thunder is no sign of a quick ear.

Ho Shih gives as real instances of strength, sharp sight and quick hearing: Wu Huo, who could lift a tripod weighing 250 stone (350 lb.); Li Chu, who at a distance of a hundred paces could see objects no bigger than a mustard seed; and Shih K'uang, a blind musician who could hear the footsteps of a mosquito.

11. What the ancients called a clever fighter is one who not only wins, but excels in winning with ease.

'He who only sees the obvious, wins his battles with difficulty; he who looks below the surface of things, wins with ease.'

12. Hence his victories bring him neither reputation for wisdom nor credit for courage.

'Inasmuch as his victories are gained over circumstances that have not come to light, the world at large knows nothing of them, and he wins no reputation for wisdom; inasmuch as the hostile state submits before there has been any bloodshed, he receives no credit for courage.'

13. He wins his battles by making no mistakes.

'He plans no superfluous marches, he devises no futile attacks. One who seeks to conquer by sheer strength,

> clever though he may be at winning pitched battles, is also
> liable on occasion to be vanquished; whereas he who can
> look into the future and discern conditions that are not yet
> manifest, will never make a blunder and therefore invariably
> win.'

Making no mistakes is what establishes the certainty of victory, for it means conquering an enemy that is already defeated.

14. Hence the skilful fighter puts himself into a position which makes defeat impossible, and does not miss the moment for defeating the enemy.

15. Thus it is that in war the victorious strategist only seeks battle after the victory has been won, whereas he who is destined to defeat first fights and afterwards looks for victory.

> 'In warfare, first lay plans which will ensure victory, and then
> lead your army to battle; if you will not begin with stratagem
> but rely on brute strength alone, victory will no longer be
> assured.'

16. The consummate leader cultivates the moral law, and strictly adheres to method and discipline; thus it is in his power to control success.

17. In respect of military method, we have, firstly, Measurement; secondly, Estimation of quantity; thirdly, Calculation; fourthly, Balancing of chances; fifthly, Victory.

18. Measurement owes its existence to Earth; Estimation of quantity to Measurement; Calculation to Estimation of quantity; Balancing of chances to Calculation; and Victory to Balancing of chances.

19. A victorious army opposed to a routed one, is as a pound's weight placed in the scale against a single grain.

20. The onrush of a conquering force is like the bursting of pent-up waters into a chasm a thousand fathoms deep. So much for tactical dispositions.

V Energy

1. Sun Tzŭ said: The control of a large force is the same in principle as the control of a few men: it is merely a question of dividing up their numbers.

2. Fighting with a large army under your command is nowise different from fighting with a small one: it is merely a question of instituting signs and signals.

3. To ensure that your whole host may withstand the brunt of the enemy's attack and remain unshaken – this is effected by manœuvres direct and indirect.

> 'We must cause the enemy to regard our straightforward attack as one that is secretly designed, and *vice versa*.'

4. That the impact of your army may be like a grind-stone dashed against an egg – this is effected by the science of weak points and strong.

5. In all fighting, the direct method may be used for joining battle, but indirect methods will be needed in order to secure victory.

> 'Steadily develop indirect tactics, either by pounding the enemy's flanks or falling on his rear.'

6. Indirect tactics, efficiently applied, are inexhaustible as Heaven and Earth, unending as the flow of rivers and streams; like the sun and moon, they end but to begin anew; like the four seasons, they pass away but to return once more.

7. There are not more than five musical notes, yet the

combinations of these five give rise to more melodies than can ever be heard.

8. There are not more than five primary colours,

   blue, yellow, red, white and black.

yet in combination they produce more hues than can ever be seen.

9. There are not more than five cardinal tastes,

   sour, acrid, salt, sweet, bitter.

yet combinations of them yield more flavours than can ever be tasted.

10. In battle, there are not more than two methods of attack – the direct and the indirect; yet these two in combination give rise to an endless series of manœuvres.

11. The direct and the indirect lead on to each other in turn. It is like moving in a circle – you never come to an end. Who can exhaust the possibilities of their combination?

12. The onset of troops is like the rush of a torrent which will even roll stones along in its course.

13. The quality of decision is like the well-timed swoop of a falcon which enables it to strike and destroy its victim.

14. Therefore the good fighter will be terrible in his onset, and prompt in his decision.

15. Energy may be likened to the bending of a crossbow; decision, to the releasing of the trigger.

16. Amid the turmoil and tumult of battle, there may be seeming disorder and yet no real disorder at all; amid confusion and chaos, your array may be without head or tail, yet it will be proof against defeat.

17. Simulated disorder postulates perfect discipline; simulated fear postulates courage; simulated weakness postulates strength.

'If you wish to feign confusion in order to lure the enemy on, you must first have perfect discipline; if you wish to display timidity in order to entrap the enemy, you must have extreme courage; if you wish to parade your weakness in order to make the enemy over-confident, you must have exceeding strength.'

18. Hiding order beneath the cloak of disorder is simply a question of subdivision; concealing courage under a show of timidity presupposes a fund of latent energy; masking strength with weakness is to be effected by tactical dispositions.

Chang Yü relates the following anecdote of Kao Tsu, the first Han Emperor: Wishing to crush the Hsiung-nu, he sent out spies to report on their condition. But the Hsiung-nu, forewarned, carefully concealed all their able-bodied men and well-fed horses, and only allowed infirm soldiers and emaciated cattle to be seen. The result was that the spies one and all recommended the Emperor to deliver his attack. Lou Ching alone opposed them, saying: 'When two countries go to war, they are naturally inclined to make an ostentatious display of their strength. Yet our spies have seen nothing but old age and infirmity. This is surely some *ruse* on the part of the enemy, and it would be unwise for us to attack.' The Emperor, however, disregarding this advice, fell into the trap and found himself surrounded at Po-têng.

19. Thus one who is skilful at keeping the enemy on the move maintains deceitful appearances, according to which the enemy will act. He sacrifices something that the enemy may snatch at it.

In 341 B.C., the Ch'i State being at war with Wei, sent T'ien Chi and Sun Pin against the general P'ang Chüan, who happened to be a deadly personal enemy of the latter. Sun Pin said: 'The Ch'i State has a reputation for cowardice, and therefore our adversary despises us. Let us turn this circumstance to account.' Accordingly, when the army had crossed the border into Wei territory, he gave orders to show 100,000 fires on the first night, 50,000 on the next, and the night after only 20,000. P'ang Chüan pursued them hotly, saying to himself: 'I knew these men of Ch'i were cowards: their numbers have already fallen away by more than half.' In his retreat, Sun Pin came to a narrow defile, which he calculated that his pursuers would reach after dark. Here he had a tree stripped of its bark, and inscribed upon it the words: 'Under this tree shall P'ang Chüan die.' Then, as night began to fall, he placed a strong body of archers in ambush near by, with orders to shoot directly they saw a light. Later on, P'ang Chüan arrived at the spot, and noticing the tree, struck a light in order to read what was written on it. His body was immediately riddled by a volley of arrows, and his whole army thrown into confusion. [The above is Tu Mu's version of the story; the *Shih Chi*, less dramatically but probably with more historical truth, makes P'ang Chüan cut his own throat with an exclamation of despair, after the rout of his army.]

20. By holding out baits, he keeps him on the march; then with a body of picked men he lies in wait for him.

21. The clever combatant looks to the effect of combined energy, and does not require too much from individuals.

'He first of all considers the power of his army in the bulk; afterwards he takes individual talent into account, and uses each man according to his capabilities. He does not demand perfection from the untalented.'

Hence his ability to pick out the right men and to utilise combined energy.

22. When he utilises combined energy, his fighting men become as it were like unto rolling logs or stones. For it is the nature of a log or stone to remain motionless on level ground, and to move when on a slope; if four-cornered, to come to a standstill, but if round-shaped, to go rolling down.

23. Thus the energy developed by good fighting men is as the momentum of a round stone rolled down a mountain thousands of feet in height. So much on the subject of energy.

The chief lesson is the paramount importance in war of rapid evolutions and sudden rushes. 'Great results can thus be achieved with small forces.'

VI Weak Points and Strong

1. Sun Tzǔ said: Whoever is first in the field and awaits the coming of the enemy, will be fresh for the fight; whoever is second in the field and has to hasten to battle, will arrive exhausted.

2. Therefore the clever combatant imposes his will on the enemy, but does not allow the enemy's will to be imposed on him.

3. By holding out advantages to him, he can cause the enemy to approach of his own accord; or, by inflicting damage, he can make it impossible for the enemy to draw near.

> In the first case, he will entice him with a bait; in the second, he will strike at some important point which the enemy will have to defend.

4. If the enemy is taking his ease, he can harass him; if well supplied with food, he can starve him out; if quietly encamped, he can force him to move.

5. Appear at points which the enemy must hasten to defend; march swiftly to places where you are not expected.

6. An army may march great distances without distress, if it marches through country where the enemy is not.

> 'Emerge from the void, strike at vulnerable points, shun places that are defended, attack in unexpected quarters.'

7. You can be sure of succeeding in your attacks if you only attack places which are undefended. You can ensure the safety

of your defence if you only hold positions that cannot be attacked.

> 'He who is skilled in attack flashes forth from the topmost heights of heaven, making it impossible for the enemy to guard against him. This being so, the places that I shall attack are precisely those that the enemy cannot defend . . . He who is skilled in defence hides in the most secret recesses of the earth, making it impossible for the enemy to estimate his whereabouts. This being so, the places that I shall hold are precisely those that the enemy cannot attack.'

8. Hence that general is skilful in attack whose opponent does not know what to defend; and he is skilful in defence whose opponent does not know what to attack.

9. O divine art of sublety and secrecy! Through you we learn to be invisible, through you inaudible and hence we can hold the enemy's fate in our hands.

10. You may advance and be absolutely irresistible, if you make for the enemy's weak points; you may retire and be safe from pursuit if your movements are more rapid than those of the enemy.

11. If we wish to fight, the enemy can be forced to an engagement even though he be sheltered behind a high rampart and a deep ditch. All we need do is to attack some other place that he will be obliged to relieve.

> 'If the enemy is the invading party, we can cut his line of communications and occupy the roads by which he will have to return; if we are the invaders, we may direct our attack against the sovereign himself.' It is clear that Sun Tzŭ was no believer in frontal attacks.

12. If we do not wish to fight, we can prevent the enemy from engaging us even though the lines of our encampment be merely

traced out on the ground. All we need do is to throw something odd and unaccountable in his way.

> Chu-ko Liang, who when occupying Yang-p'ing and about to be attacked by Ssŭ-ma I, suddenly struck his colours, stopped the beating of the drums, and flung open the city gates, showing only a few men engaged in sweeping and sprinkling the ground. This unexpected proceeding had the intended effect; for Ssŭ-ma I, suspecting an ambush, actually drew off his army and retreated. What Sun Tzŭ is advocating here, therefore, is nothing more nor less than the timely use of 'bluff.'

13. By discovering the enemy's dispositions and remaining invisible ourselves, we can keep our forces concentrated, while the enemy's must be divided.

> 'If the enemy's dispositions are visible, we can make for him in one body; whereas, our own dispositions being kept secret, the enemy will be obliged to divide his forces in order to guard against attack from every quarter.'

14. We can form a single united body, while the enemy must split up into fractions. Hence there will be a whole pitted against separate parts of a whole, which means that we shall be many to the enemy's few.

15. And if we are able thus to attack an inferior force with a superior one, our opponents will be in dire straits.

16. The spot where we intend to fight must not be made known; for then the enemy will have to prepare against a possible attack at several different points;

> Sheridan once explained the reason of General Grant's victories by saying that 'while his opponents were kept fully employed wondering what he was going to do, *he* was thinking most of what he was going to do himself.'

and his forces being thus distributed in many directions, the numbers we shall have to face at any given point will be proportionately few.

17. For should the enemy strengthen his van, he will weaken his rear; should he strengthen his rear, he will weaken his van; should he strengthen his left, he will weaken his right; should he strengthen his right, he will weaken his left. If he sends reinforcements everywhere, he will everywhere be weak.

'A defensive war is apt to betray us into too frequent detachment. Those generals who have had but little experience attempt to protect every point, while those who are better acquainted with their profession, having only the capital object in view, guard against a decisive blow, and acquiesce in smaller misfortunes to avoid greater.'

18. Numerical weakness comes from having to prepare against possible attacks; numerical strength, from compelling our adversary to make these preparations against us.

The highest generalship is 'to compel the enemy to disperse his army, and then to concentrate superior force against each fraction in turn.'

19. Knowing the place and the time of the coming battle, we may concentrate from the greatest distances in order to fight.

20. But if neither time nor place be known, then the left wing will be impotent to succour the right, the right equally impotent to succour the left, the van unable to relieve the rear, or the rear to support the van. How much more so if the furthest portions of the army are anything under a hundred *li* apart, and even the nearest are separated by several *li*!

The mental picture we are required to draw is that of an army advancing towards a given rendezvous in separate columns, each of which has orders to be there on a fixed date. If the general allows the various detachments to proceed at haphazard, without precise instructions as to the time and place of meeting, the enemy will be able to annihilate the army in detail. 'If we do not know the place where our opponents mean to concentrate or the day on which they will join battle, our unity will be forfeited through our preparations for defence, and the positions we hold will be insecure. Suddenly happening upon a powerful foe, we shall be brought to battle in a flurried condition, and no mutual support will be possible between wings, vanguard or rear, especially if there is any great distance between the foremost and hindmost divisions of the army.'

21. Though according to my estimate the soldiers of Yüeh exceed our own in number, that shall advantage them nothing in the matter of victory. I say then that victory can be achieved.

22. Though the enemy be stronger in numbers, we may prevent him from fighting. Scheme so as to discover his plans and the likelihood of their success.

23. Rouse him, and learn the principle of his activity or inactivity.

Chang Yü tells us that by noting the joy or anger shown by the enemy on being thus disturbed, we shall be able to conclude whether his policy is to lie low or the reverse. He instances the action of Chu-ko Liang, who sent the scornful present of a woman's head-dress to Ssŭ-ma I, in order to goad him out of his Fabian tactics.

Force him to reveal himself, so as to find out his vulnerable spots.

24. Carefully compare the opposing army with your own, so that you may know where strength is super-abundant and where it is deficient.

25. In making tactical dispositions, the highest pitch you can attain is to conceal them; conceal your dispositions, and you will be safe from the prying of the subtlest spies, from the machinations of the wisest brains.

26. How victory may be produced for them out of the enemy's own tactics – that is what the multitude cannot comprehend.

27. All men can see the tactics whereby I conquer, but what none can see is the strategy out of which victory is evolved.

28. Do not repeat the tactics which have gained you one victory, but let your methods be regulated by the infinite variety of circumstances.

> 'There is but one root-principle underlying victory, but the tactics which lead up to it are infinite in number.' The rules of strategy are few and simple. They may be learned in a week. They may be taught by familiar illustrations or a dozen diagrams. But such knowledge will no more teach a man to lead an army like Napoleon than a knowledge of grammar will teach him to write like Gibbon.

29. Military tactics are like unto water; for water in its natural course runs away from high places and hastens downwards.

30. So in war, the way is to avoid what is strong and to strike at what is weak.

> Like water, taking the line of least resistance.

31. Water shapes its course according to the nature of the ground over which it flows; the soldier works out his victory in relation to the foe whom he is facing.

32. Therefore, just as water retains no constant shape, so in warfare there are no constant conditions. The five elements: Water, fire, wood, metal, earth, are not always equally predominant; the four seasons make way for each other in turn. There

are short days and long; the moon has its periods of waning and waxing.

33. He who can modify his tactics in relation to his opponent and thereby succeed in winning, may be called a heaven-born captain.

VII Manoeuvring

1. Sun Tzŭ said: In war, the general receives his commands from the sovereign.

2. Having collected an army and concentrated his forces, he must blend and harmonise the different elements thereof before pitching his camp.

> 'Without harmony in the State, no military expedition can be undertaken; without harmony in the army, no battle array can be formed.'

3. After that, comes tactical manœuvring, than which there is nothing more difficult. The difficulty of tactical manœuvring consists in turning the devious into the direct, and misfortune into gain.

> 'Make it appear that you are a long way off, then cover the distance rapidly and arrive on the scene before your opponent. Hoodwink the enemy, so that he may be remiss and leisurely while you are dashing along with the utmost speed. Although you may have difficult ground to traverse and natural obstacles to encounter, this is a drawback which can be turned into actual advantage by celerity of movement.' Signal examples of this saying are afforded by the two famous passages across the Alps – that of Hannibal, which laid Italy at his mercy, and that of Napoleon two thousand years later, which resulted in the great victory of Marengo.

4. Thus, to take a long and circuitous route, after enticing the enemy out of the way, and though starting after him, to contrive

to reach the goal before him, shows knowledge of the artifice of *deviation*.

> Tu Mu cites the famous march of Chao Shê in 270 B.C. to relieve the town of O-yü, which was closely invested by a Ch'in army. The King of Chao first consulted Lien P'o on the advisability of attempting a relief, but the latter thought the distance too great, and the intervening country too rugged and difficult. His Majesty then turned to Chao Shê, who fully admitted the hazardous nature of the march, but finally said: 'We shall be like two rats fighting in a hole – and the pluckier one will win!' So he left the capital with his army, but had only gone a distance of 30 *li* when he stopped and began throwing up intrenchments. For 28 days he continued strengthening his fortifications, and took care that spies should carry the intelligence to the enemy. The Ch'in general was overjoyed, and attributed his adversary's tardiness to the fact that the beleaguered city was in the Han State, and thus not actually part of Chao territory. But the spies had no sooner departed than Chao Shê began a forced march lasting for two days and one night, and arrived on the scene of action with such astonishing rapidity that he was able to occupy a commanding position on the 'North hill' before the enemy had got wind of his movements. A crushing defeat followed for the Ch'in forces, who were obliged to raise the siege of O-yü in all haste and retreat across the border.

5. Manœuvring with an army is advantageous; with an undisciplined multitude, most dangerous.

6. If you set a fully equipped army to march in order to snatch an advantage, the chances are that you will be too late. On the other hand, to detach a flying column for the purpose involves the sacrifice of its baggage and stores.

7. Thus, if you order your men to roll up their buff-coats, and make forced marches without halting day or night, covering

double the usual distance at a stretch, doing a hundred *li* in order to wrest an advantage, the leaders of all your three divisions will fall into the hands of the enemy.

8. The stronger men will be in front, the jaded ones will fall behind, and on this plan only one-tenth of your army will reach its destination.

> The moral is, Don't march a hundred *li* to gain a tactical advantage, either with or without impedimenta. Manœuvres of this description should be confined to short distances. Stonewall Jackson said: 'The hardships of forced marches are often more painful than the dangers of battle.' He did not often call upon his troops for extraordinary exertions. It was only when he intended a surprise, or when a rapid retreat was imperative, that he sacrificed everything to speed.

9. If you march fifty *li* in order to outmanœuvre the enemy, you will lose the leader of your first division, and only half your force will reach the goal.

10. If you march thirty *li* with the same object, two-thirds of your army will arrive.

11. We may take it then that an army without its baggage-train is lost; without provisions it is lost; without bases of supply it is lost.

12. We cannot enter into alliances until we are acquainted with the designs of our neighbours.

13. We are not fit to lead an army on the march unless we are familiar with the face of the country – its mountains and forests, its pitfalls and precipices, its marshes and swamps.

14. We shall be unable to turn natural advantages to account unless we make use of local guides.

15. In war, practise dissimulation, and you will succeed. Move only if there is a real advantage to be gained.

16. Whether to concentrate or to divide your troops, must be decided by circumstances.

17. Let your rapidity be that of the wind, your compactness that of the forest.

18. In raiding and plundering be like fire, in immovability like a mountain.

> That is, when holding a position from which the enemy is trying to dislodge you, or when he is trying to entice you into a trap.

19. Let your plans be dark and impenetrable as night, and when you move, fall like a thunderbolt.

> 'You cannot shut your ears to the thunder or your eyes to the lighting – so rapid are they.' Likewise, an attack should be made so quickly that it cannot be parried.

20. When you plunder a countryside, let the spoil be divided amongst your men; when you capture new territory, cut it up into allotments for the benefit of the soldiery.

21. Ponder and deliberate before you make a move.

22. He will conquer who has learnt the artifice of deviation. Such is the art of manœuvring.

23. The Book of Army Management says: On the field of battle, the spoken word does not carry far enough: hence the institution of gongs and drums. Nor can ordinary objects be seen clearly enough: hence the institution of banners and flags.

24. Gongs and drums, banners and flags, are means whereby the ears and eyes of the host may be focused on one particular point.

25. The host thus forming a single united body, it is impossible either for the brave to advance alone, or for the cowardly to retreat alone.

'Equally guilty are those who advance against orders and those who retreat against orders.' Tu Mu tells a story in this connection of Wu Ch'i, when he was fighting against the Ch'in State. Before the battle had begun, one of his soldiers, a man of matchless daring, sallied forth by himself, captured two heads from the enemy, and returned to camp. Wu Ch'i had the man instantly executed, where-upon an officer ventured to remonstrate saying: 'This man was a good soldier, and ought not to have been beheaded.' Wu Ch'i replied: 'I fully believe he was a good soldier, but I had him beheaded because he acted without orders.'

This is the art of handling large masses of men.

26. In night-fighting, then, make much use of signal-fires and drums, and in fighting by day, of flags and banners, as a means of influencing the ears and eyes of your army.

27. A whole army may be robbed of its spirit;

'In war, if a spirit of anger can be made to pervade all ranks of an army at one and the same time, its onset will be irre-sistible. Now the spirit of the enemy's soldiers will be keenest when they have newly arrived on the scene, and it is there-fore our cue not to fight at once, but to wait until their ardour and enthusiasm have worn off, and then strike. It is in this way that they may be robbed of their keen spirit.' Li Ch'üan and others tell an anecdote of Ts'ao Kuei, a *protégé* of Duke Chuang of Lu. The latter State was attacked by Ch'i, and the Duke was about to join battle at Ch'ang-cho, after the first roll of the enemy's drums, when Ts'ao said: 'Not just yet.' Only after their drums had beaten for the third time, did he give the word for attack. Then they fought, and the men of

Ch'i were utterly defeated. Questioned afterwards by the Duke as to the meaning of his delay, Ts'ao Kuei replied: 'In battle, a courageous spirit is everything. Now the first roll of the drum tends to create this spirit, but with the second it is already on the wane, and after the third it is gone altogether. I attacked when their spirit was gone and ours was at its height. Hence our victory. The value of a whole army – a mighty host of a million men – is dependent on one man alone: such is the influence of spirit!'

a commander-in-chief may be robbed of his presence of mind.

'Presence of mind is the general's most important asset. It is the quality which enables him to discipline disorder and to inspire courage into the panic-stricken.' The great general Li Ching (A.D. 571–649) has a saying: 'Attacking does not merely consist in assaulting walled cities or striking at an army in battle array; it must include the art of assailing the enemy's mental equilibrium.'

28. Now a soldier's spirit is keenest in the morning;

Always provided, I suppose, that he has had breakfast. At the battle of the Trebia, the Romans were foolishly allowed to fight fasting, whereas Hannibal's men had breakfasted at their leisure.

by noonday it has begun to flag; and in the evening, his mind is bent only on returning to camp.

29. A clever general, therefore, avoids an army when its spirit is keen, but attacks it when it is sluggish and inclined to return. This is the art of studying moods.

30. Disciplined and calm, to await the appearance of disorder and hubbub amongst the enemy – this is the art of retaining self-possession.

31. To be near the goal while the enemy is still far from it, to

wait at ease while the enemy is toiling and struggling, to be well-fed while the enemy is famished – this is the art of husbanding one's strength.

32. To refrain from intercepting an enemy whose banners are in perfect order, to refrain from attacking an army drawn up in calm and confident array – this is the art of studying circumstances.

33. It is a military axiom not to advance uphill against the enemy, nor to oppose him when he comes downhill.

34. Do not pursue an enemy who simulates flight; do not attack soldiers whose temper is keen.

35. Do not swallow a bait offered by the enemy. Do not interfere with an army that is returning home.

The commentators explain this rather singular piece of advice by saying that a man whose heart is set on returning home will fight to the death against any attempt to bar his way, and is therefore too dangerous an opponent to be tackled. 'Invincible is the soldier who hath his desire and returneth homewards.' A marvellous tale is told of Ts'ao Ts'ao's courage and resource: In A.D. 198, he was besieging Chang Hsiu in Jang, when Liu Piao sent reinforcements with a view to cutting off Ts'ao's retreat. The latter was obliged to draw off his troops, only to find himself hemmed in between two enemies, who were guarding each outlet of a narrow pass in which he had engaged himself. In this desperate plight Ts'ao waited until nightfall, when he bored a tunnel into the mountain side and laid an ambush in it. Then he marched on with his baggage-train, and when it grew light, Chang Hsiu, finding that the bird had flown, pressed after him in hot pursuit. As soon as the whole army had passed by, the hidden troops fell on its rear, while Ts'ao himself turned and met his pursuers in front, so that they were thrown into confusion and annihilated. Ts'ao Ts'ao said afterwards: 'The brigands tried to check my army in its retreat and brought me to battle in a desperate position: hence I knew how to overcome them.'

36. When you surround an army, leave an outlet free.

This does not mean that the enemy is to be allowed to escape. The object is 'to make him believe that there is a road to safety, and thus prevent his fighting with the courage of despair.' Tu Mu adds pleasantly: 'After that, you may crush him.'

Do not press a desperate foe too hard.

'Birds and beasts when brought to bay will use their claws and teeth. If your adversary has burned his boats and destroyed his cooking-pots, and is ready to stake all on the issue of a battle, he must not be pushed to extremities.' Ho Shih illustrates the meaning by a story taken from the life of Fu Yen-Ch'ing. That general was surrounded by a vastly superior army of Khitans in the year A.D. 945. The country was bare and desert-like, and the little Chinese force was soon in dire straits for want of water. The wells they bored ran dry, and the men were reduced to squeezing lumps of mud and sucking out the moisture. Their ranks thinned rapidly, until at last Fu Yen-Ch'ing exclaimed: 'We are desperate men. Far better to die for our country than to go with fettered hands into captivity!' A strong gale happened to be blowing from the north-east and darkening the air with dense clouds of sandy dust. Tu Chung-wei was for waiting until this had abated before deciding on a final attack; but luckily another officer, Li Shou-chêng by name, was quicker to see an opportunity, and said: 'They are many and we are few, but in the midst of this sandstorm our numbers will not be discernible; victory will go to the strenuous fighter, and the wind will be our best ally.' Accordingly, Fu Yen-Ch'ing made a sudden and wholly unexpected onslaught with his cavalry, routed the barbarians and succeeded in breaking through to safety.

37. Such is the art of warfare.

VIII Variation of Tactics

1. Sun Tzǔ said: In war, the general receives his commands from the sovereign, collects his army and concentrates his forces.

2. When in difficult country, do not encamp. In country where high roads intersect, join hands with your allies. Do not linger in dangerously isolated positions. In hemmed-in situations, you must resort to stratagem. In a desperate position, you must fight.

3. There are roads which must not be followed,

> 'Especially those leading through narrow defiles,' says Li Ch'üan, 'where an ambush is to be feared.'

armies which must not be attacked,

> More correctly, perhaps, there are times when an army must not be attacked. 'When you see your way to obtain a trivial advantage, but are powerless to inflict a real defeat, refrain from attacking, for fear of overtaxing your men's strength.'

towns which must not be besieged,

> Ts'ao Kung gives an interesting illustration from his own experience. When invading the territory of Hsü-chou, he ignored the city of Hua-pi, which lay directly in his path, and pressed on into the heart of the country. This excellent strategy was rewarded by the subsequent capture of no fewer than fourteen important district cities. 'No town should be attacked which, if taken, cannot be held, or if left alone, will not cause any trouble.' Hsün Ying, when urged to attack Pi-yang, replied:

> 'The city is small and well-fortified; even if I succeed in taking it, it will be no great feat of arms; whereas if I fail, I shall make myself a laughing-stock. It is a great mistake to waste men in taking a town when the same expenditure of soldiers will gain a province.'

positions which must not be contested, commands of the sovereign which must not be obeyed.

> 'Even if it be your sovereign's command to encamp in difficult country, linger in isolated positions, etc., you must not do so.'

4. The general who thoroughly understands the advantages that accompany variation of tactics knows how to handle his troops.

5. The general who does not understand these, may be well acquainted with the configuration of the country, yet he will not be able to turn his knowledge to practical account.

6. So, the student of war who is unversed in the art of varying his plans, even though he be acquainted with the Five Advantages, will fail to make the best use of his men.

7. Hence in the wise leader's plans, considerations of advantage and of disadvantage will be blended together.

8. If our expectation of advantage be tempered in this way, we may succeed in accomplishing the essential part of our schemes.

> 'If we wish to wrest an advantage from the enemy, we must not fix our minds on that alone, but allow for the possibility of the enemy also doing some harm to us, and let this enter as a factor into our calculations.'

9. If, on the other hand, in the midst of difficulties we are always ready to seize an advantage, we may extricate ourselves from misfortune.

> 'If I wish to extricate myself from a dangerous position, I must

consider not only the enemy's ability to injure me, but also my own ability to gain an advantage over the enemy. If in my counsels these two considerations are properly blended, I shall succeed in liberating myself . . . For instance, if I am surrounded by the enemy and only think of effecting an escape, the nervelessness of my policy will incite my adversary to pursue and crush me; it would be far better to encourage my men to deliver a bold counter-attack, and use the advantage thus gained to free myself from the enemy's toils. The wise man considers well both advantage and disadvantage. He sees a way out of adversity, *and on the day of victory is not blind to danger.'*

10. Reduce the hostile chiefs by inflicting damage on them;

Chia Lin enumerates several ways of inflicting this injury: 'Entice away the enemy's best and wisest men, so that he may be left without counsellors. Introduce traitors into his country, that the government policy may be rendered futile. Foment intrigue and deceit, and thus sow dissension between the ruler and his ministers. By means of every artful contrivance, cause deterioration amongst his men and waste of his treasure. Corrupt his morals by insidious gifts leading him into excess. Disturb and unsettle his mind by presenting him with lovely women.' *Isn't this precisely what is being done to us?*

make trouble for them, and keep them constantly engaged; hold out specious allurements, and make them rush to any given point.

11. The art of war teaches us to rely not on the likelihood of the enemy's not coming, but on our own readiness to receive him; not on the chance of his not attacking, but rather on the fact that we have made our position unassailable.

12. There are five dangerous faults which may affect a general;

(1) Recklessness, which leads to destruction; (2) cowardice, which leads to capture;

Sun Tzŭ knew nothing is to be achieved in war unless you are willing to take risks. In A.D. 404, Liu Yü pursued the rebel Huan Hsüan up the Yangtsze and fought a naval battle with him at the island of Ch'êng-hung. The loyal troops numbered only a few thousands, while their opponents were in great force. But Huan Hsüan, fearing the fate which was in store for him should he be overcome, had a light boat made fast to the side of his war-junk, so that he might escape, if necessary, at a moment's notice. The natural result was that the fighting spirit of his soldiers was utterly quenched, and when the loyalists made an attack from windward with fireships, all striving with the utmost ardour to be first in the fray, Huan Hsüan's forces were routed, had to burn all their baggage and fled for two days and nights without stopping.

(3) a hasty temper, which can be provoked by insults;

Yao Hsiang, when opposed in A.D. 357 by Huang Mei, Têng Ch'iang and others, shut himself up behind his walls and refused to fight. Têng Ch'iang said: 'Our adversary is of a choleric temper and easily provoked; let us make constant sallies and break down his walls, then he will grow angry and come out. Once we can bring his force to battle, it is doomed to be our prey.' This plan was acted upon, Yao Hsiang came out to fight, was lured on as far as San-yüan by the enemy's pretended flight, and finally attacked and slain.

(4) a delicacy of honour which is sensitive to shame;

'The seeker after glory should be careless of public opinion.'

(5) over-solicitude for his men, which exposes him to worry and trouble.

Here again, Sun Tzŭ does not mean that the general is to be careless of the welfare of his troops. All he wishes to emphasise is the danger of sacrificing any important military advantage to the immediate comfort of his men. This is a shortsighted policy, because in the long run the troops will suffer more from the defeat, or, at best, the prolongation of the war, which will be the consequence. A mistaken feeling of pity will often induce a general to relieve a beleaguered city, or to reinforce a hard-pressed detachment, contrary to his military instincts.

13. These are the five besetting sins of a general, ruinous to the conduct of war. When an army is overthrown and its leader slain, the cause will surely be found among these five dangerous faults. Let them be a subject of meditation.

IX The Army on the March

1. Sun Tzŭ said: We come now to the question of encamping the army, and observing signs of the enemy. Pass quickly over mountains, and keep in the neighbourhood of valleys.

'Wu-tu Ch'iang was a robber captain in the time of the Later Han, and Ma Yüan was sent to exterminate his gang. Ch'iang having found a refuge in the hills, Ma Yüan made no attempt to force a battle, but seized all the favourable positions commanding supplies of water and forage. Ch'iang was soon in such a desperate plight for want of provisions that he was forced to make a total surrender. He did not know the advantage of keeping in the neighbourhood of valleys.'

2. Camp in high places,

Not on high hills, but on knolls or hillocks elevated above the surrounding country.

facing the sun. Do not climb heights in order to fight. So much for mountain warfare.

3. After crossing a river, you should get far away from it.

4. When an invading force crosses a river in its onward march, do not advance to meet it in mid-stream. It will be best to let half the army get across, and then deliver your attack.

Li Ch'üan alludes to the great victory won by Han Hsin over Lung Chü at the Wei River. 'The two armies were drawn up on opposite sides of the river. In the night, Han Hsin ordered his men to take some ten thousand sacks filled with sand and construct a dam a little higher up. Then, leading half his army across, he attacked Lung Chü; but after a time, pretending to have failed in his attempt, he hastily withdrew to the other bank. Lung Chü was much elated by this unlooked-for success, and exclaiming: 'I felt sure that Han Hsin was really a coward!' he pursued him and began crossing the river in his turn. Han Hsin now sent a party to cut open the sandbags, thus releasing a great volume of water, which swept down and prevented the greater portion of Lung Chü's army from getting across. He then turned upon the force which had been cut off, and annihilated it, Lung Chü himself being amongst the slain. The rest of the army, on the further bank, also scattered and fled in all directions.'

5. If you are anxious to fight, you should not go to meet the invader near a river which he has to cross.

6. Moor your craft higher up than the enemy, and facing the sun. Do not move up-stream to meet the enemy.

'As water flows downwards, we must not pitch our camp on the lower reaches of a river, for fear the enemy should open the sluices and sweep us away in a flood. In river warfare we must not advance against the stream, which is as much as to say that our fleet must not be anchored below that of the enemy, for then they would be able to take advantage of the current and make short work of us.'

So much for river warfare.

7. In crossing salt-marshes, your sole concern should be to get over them quickly, without any delay.

Because of the lack of fresh water, the poor quality of the herbage, and last but not least, because they are low, flat, and exposed to attack.

54

8. If forced to fight in a salt-marsh, you should have water and grass near you, and get your back to a clump of trees.

> Li Ch'üan remarks that the ground is less likely to be treacherous where there are trees, while Tu Yu says that they will serve to protect the rear.

So much for operations in salt-marshes.

9. In dry, level country, take up an easily accessible position with rising ground to your right and on your rear, so that the danger may be in front, and safety lie behind. So much for campaigning in flat country.

10. These are the four useful branches of military knowledge which enabled the Yellow Emperor to vanquish four several sovereigns.

11. All armies prefer high ground to low, and sunny places to dark.

> 'High ground is not only more agreeable and salubrious, but more convenient from a military point of view; low ground is not only damp and unhealthy, but also disadvantageous for fighting.'

12. If you are careful of your men, and camp on hard ground, the army will be free from disease of every kind, and this will spell victory.

13. When you come to a hill or a bank, occupy the sunny side, with the slope on your right rear. Thus you will at once act for the benefit of your soldiers and utilise the natural advantages of the ground.

14. When, in consequence of heavy rains up-country, a river which you wish to ford is swollen and flecked with foam, you must wait until it subsides.

15. Country in which there are precipitous cliffs with torrents

running between, deep natural hollows, confined places, tangled thickets, quagmires and crevasses, should be left with all possible speed and not approached.

16. While we keep away from such places, we should get the enemy to approach them; while we face them, we should let the enemy have them on his rear.

17. If in the neighbourhood of your camp there should be any hilly country, ponds surrounded by aquatic grass, hollow basins filled with reeds, or woods with thick undergrowth, they must be carefully routed out and searched; for these are places where men in ambush or insidious spies are likely to be lurking.

18. When the enemy is close at hand and remains quiet, he is relying on the natural strength of his position.

19. When he keeps aloof and tries to provoke a battle, he is anxious for the other side to advance.

20. If his place of encampment is easy of access, he is tendering a bait.

21. Movement amongst the trees of a forest shows that the enemy is advancing.

'Every army sends out scouts to climb high places and observe the enemy. If a scout sees that the trees of a forest are moving and shaking, he may know that they are being cut down to clear a passage for the enemy's march.'

The appearance of a number of screens in the midst of thick grass means that the enemy wants to make us suspicious.

22. The rising of birds in their flight is the sign of an ambuscade.

'When birds that are flying along in a straight line suddenly shoot upwards, it means that soldiers are in ambush at the spot beneath.'

Startled beasts indicate that a sudden attack is coming.

23. When there is dust rising in a high column, it is the sign of chariots advancing; when the dust is low, but spread over a wide area, it betokens the approach of infantry. When it branches out in different directions, it shows that parties have been sent to collect firewood. A few clouds of dust moving to and fro signify that the army is encamping.

> 'As you move along, say, in a hostile country, your eyes should be looking afar for the enemy or any signs of him: figures, dust rising, birds getting up, glitter of arms, etc.'

24. Humble words and increased preparations are signs that the enemy is about to advance. Violent language and driving forward as if to the attack are signs that he will retreat.

> Chang Yü alludes to the story of T'ien Tan of the Ch'i State, who in 279 B.C. was hard-pressed in his defence of Chi-mo against the Yen forces, led by Ch'i Chieh. 'Tien Tan openly said: "My only fear is that the Yen army may cut off the noses of their Ch'i prisoners and place them in the front rank to fight against us; that would be the undoing of our city." The other side being informed of this speech, at once acted on the suggestion; but those within the city were enraged at seeing their fellow-countrymen thus mutilated, and fearing only lest they should fall into the enemy's hands, were nerved to defend themselves more obstinately than ever. Once again T'ien Tan sent back converted spies who reported these words to the enemy: 'What I dread most is that the men of Yen may dig up the ancestral tombs outside the town, and by inflicting this indignity on our forefathers cause us to become faint-hearted.' Forthwith the besiegers dug up all the graves and burned the corpses lying in them. And the inhabitants of Chi-mo, witnessing the outrage from the city-walls, wept passionately and were all impatient to go out and fight, their fury being increased tenfold. T'ien Tan knew then that

his soldiers were ready for any enterprise. But instead of a sword, he himself took a mattock in his hands, and ordered others to be distributed amongst his best warriors, while the ranks were filled up with their wives and concubines. He then served out all the remaining rations and bade his men eat their fill. The regular soldiers were told to keep out of sight, and the walls were manned with the old and weaker men and with women. This done, envoys were despatched to the enemy's camp to arrange terms of surrender, whereupon the Yen army began shouting for joy. T'ien Tan also collected 20,000 ounces of silver from the people, and got the wealthy citizens of Chi-mo to send it to the Yen general with the prayer that, when the town capitulated, he would not allow their homes to be plundered or their women to be maltreated. Ch'i Chieh, in high good humour, granted their prayer; but his army now became increasingly slack and careless. Meanwhile, T'ien Tan got together a thousand oxen, decked them with pieces of red silk, painted their bodies, dragon-like, with coloured stripes, and fastened sharp blades on their horns and well-greased rushes on their tails. When night came on, he lighted the ends of the rushes, and drove the oxen through a number of holes which he had pierced in the walls, backing them up with a force of 5000 picked warriors. The animals, maddened with pain, dashed furiously into the enemy's camp where they caused the utmost confusion and dismay; for their tails acted as torches, showing up the hideous pattern on their bodies, and the weapons on their horns killed or wounded any with whom they came into contact. In the meantime, the band of 5000 had crept up with gags in their mouths, and now threw themselves on the enemy. At the same moment a frightful din arose in the city itself, all those that remained behind making as much noise as possible by banging drums and hammering on bronze vessels, until heaven and earth were convulsed by the uproar. Terror-stricken, the Yen army fled in disorder, hotly pursued by the men of Ch'i, who succeeded in slaying their general Ch'i Chieh ... The result of the battle was the ultimate recovery of some seventy cities which had belonged to the Ch'i State.'

25. When the light chariots come out first and take up a position on the wings, it is a sign that the enemy is forming for battle.

26. Peace proposals unaccompanied by a sworn covenant indicate a plot.

27. When there is much running about and the soldiers fall into rank, it means that the critical moment has come.

28. When some are seen advancing and some retreating, it is a lure.

29. When the soldiers stand leaning on their spears, they are faint from want of food.

30. If those who are sent to draw water begin by drinking themselves, the army is suffering from thirst.

31. If the enemy sees an advantage to be gained and makes no effort to secure it, the soldiers are exhausted.

32. If birds gather on any spot, it is unoccupied.

A useful fact to bear in mind when, for instance, the enemy has secretly abandoned his camp.

Clamour by night betokens nervousness.

'Fear makes men restless; so they fall to shouting at night in order to keep up their courage.'

33. If there is disturbance in the camp, the general's authority is weak. If the banners and flags are shifted about, sedition is afoot. If the officers are angry, it means that the men are weary.

34. When an army feeds its horses with grain and kills its cattle

for food, and when the men do not hang their cooking-pots over the camp-fires, showing that they will not return to their tents, you may know that they are determined to fight to the death.

'The rebel Wang Kuo of Liang was besieging the town of Ch'ên-ts'ang, and Huang-fu Sung, who was in supreme command, and Tung Cho were sent out against him. The latter pressed for hasty measures, but Sung turned a deaf ear to his counsel. At last the rebels were utterly worn out, and began to throw down their weapons of their own accord. Sung was now for advancing to the attack, but Cho said: "It is a principle of war not to pursue desperate men and not to press a retreating host." Sung answered: "That does not apply here. What I am about to attack is a jaded army, not a retreating host; with disciplined troops I am falling on a disorganised multitude, not a band of desperate men." Thereupon he advanced to the attack unsupported by his colleague, and routed the enemy, Wang Kuo being slain.'

35. The sight of men whispering together in small knots or speaking in subdued tones points to disaffection amongst the rank and file.

36. Too frequent rewards signify that the enemy is at the end of his resources;

Because, when an army is hard pressed, there is always a fear of mutiny, and lavish rewards are given to keep the men in good temper.

too many punishments betray a condition of dire distress.

Because in such case discipline becomes relaxed, and unwonted severity is necessary to keep the men to their duty.

37. To begin by bluster, but afterwards to take fright at the enemy's numbers, shows a supreme lack of intelligence.

38. When envoys are sent with compliments in their mouths, it is a sign that the enemy wishes for a truce.

> 'If the enemy open friendly relations by sending hostages, it is a sign that they are anxious for an armistice, either because their strength is exhausted or for some other reason.'

39. If the enemy's troops march up angrily and remain facing ours for a long time without either joining battle or taking demands off again, the situation is one that demands great vigilance and circumspection.

40. If our troops are no more in number than the enemy, that is amply sufficient; it only means that no direct attack can be made.

> Literally, 'no martial advance.' That is to say, '*chêng*' tactics and frontal attacks must be eschewed, and stratagem resorted to instead.

What we can do is simply to concentrate all our available strength, keep a close watch on the enemy, and obtain reinforcements.

41. He who exercises no forethought but makes light of his opponents is sure to be captured by them.

> 'If bees and scorpions carry poison, how much more will a hostile state! Even a puny opponent, then, should not be treated with contempt.'

42. If soldiers are punished before they have grown attached to you, they will not prove submissive; and, unless submissive, they will be practically useless. If, when the soldiers have become attached to you, punishments are not enforced, they will still be useless.

43. Therefore soldiers must be treated in the first instance with humanity, but kept under control by means of iron discipline.

> Yen Tzŭ [493 B.C.] said of Ssŭ-ma Jang-cnü 'His civil virtues endeared him to the people; his martial prowess kept his enemies in awe. The ideal commander unites culture with a warlike temper; the profession of arms requires a combination of hardness and tenderness.'

This is a certain road to victory.

44. If in training soldiers commands are habitually enforced, the army will be well-disciplined; if not, its discipline will be bad.

45. If a general shows confidence in his men but always insists on his orders being obeyed, the gain will be mutual.

> 'A general ought in time of peace to show kindly confidence in his men and also make his authority respected, so that when they come to face the enemy, orders may be executed and discipline maintained, because they all trust and look up to him. The art of giving orders is not to try to rectify the minor blunders and not to be swayed by petty doubts. Vacillation and fussiness are the surest means of sapping the confidence of an army.'

X Terrain

1. Sun Tzŭ said: We may distinguish six kinds of terrain, to wit: (1) Accessible ground; (2) entangling ground; (3) temporising ground; (4) narrow passes; (5) precipitous heights; (6) positions at a great distance from the enemy.

2. Ground which can be freely traversed by both sides is called *accessible*.

3. With regard to ground of this nature, be before the enemy in occupying the raised and sunny spots, and carefully guard your line of supplies. Then you will be able to fight with advantage.

> 'The secret of war lies in the communications. The line of supply may be said to be as vital to the existence of an army as the heart to the life of a human being. Just as the duellist who finds his adversary's point menacing him with certain death, and his own guard astray, is compelled to conform to his adversary's movements, and to content himself with warding off his thrusts, so the commander whose communications are suddenly threatened finds himself in a false position, and he will be fortunate if he has not to change all his plans, to split up his force into more or less isolated detachments, and to fight with inferior numbers on ground which he has not had time to prepare, and where defeat will not be an ordinary failure, but will entail the ruin or the surrender of his whole army.'

4. Ground which can be abandoned but is hard to re-occupy is called *entangling*.

5. From a position of this sort, if the enemy is unprepared, you may sally forth and defeat him. But if the enemy is prepared for your coming, and you fail to defeat him, then, return being impossible, disaster will ensue.

6. When the position is such that neither side will gain by making the first move, it is called *temporising* ground.

'Each side finds it inconvenient to move, and the situation remains at a deadlock'

7. In a position of this sort, even though the enemy should offer us an attractive bait, it will be advisable not to stir forth, but rather to retreat, thus enticing the enemy in his turn; then, when part of his army has come out, we may deliver our attack with advantage.

8. With regard to *narrow passes*, if you can occupy them first, let them be strongly garrisoned and await the advent of the enemy.

Because then, 'the initiative will lie with us, and by making sudden and unexpected attacks we shall have the enemy at our mercy.'

9. Should the enemy forestall you in occupying a pass, do not go after him if the pass is fully garrisoned, but only if it is weakly garrisoned.

10. With regard to *precipitous heights*, if you are before-hand with your adversary, you should occupy the raised and sunny spots, and there wait for him to come up.

'The particular advantage of securing heights and defiles is that your actions cannot then be dictated by the enemy.' Chang Yü tells the following anecdote of P'ei Hsing-chien (A.D. 619–682), who was sent on a punitive expedition against the Turkic tribes. 'At nightfall he pitched his camp as usual, and it had already been completely fortified by wall and ditch, when suddenly he gave orders that the army should shift its quarters to a hill near by. This was highly displeasing to his officers, who protested loudly against the extra fatigue which it would entail on the men. P'ei Hsing-chien, however, paid no heed to their remonstrances and had the camp moved as quickly as possible. The same night, a terrific storm came on, which flooded their former place of encampment to the depth of over twelve feet. The recal-citrant officers were amazed at the sight, and owned that they had been in the wrong. 'How did you know what was going to happen?' they asked. P'ei Hsing-chien replied: 'From this time forward be content to obey orders without asking unnecessary questions." From this it may be seen that high and sunny places are advantageous not only for fighting, but also because they are immune from disastrous floods.'

11. If the enemy has occupied them before you, do not follow him, but retreat and try to entice him away.

12. If you are situated at a great distance from the enemy, and the strength of the two armies is equal, it is not easy to provoke a battle, and fighting will be to your disadvantage.

13. These six are the principles connected with Earth. The general who has attained a responsible post must be careful to study them.

14. Now an army is exposed to six several calamities, not arising from natural causes, but from faults for which the general is responsible. These are: (1) Flight; (2) in-subordination; (3) collapse; (4) ruin; (5) disorganisation; (6) rout.

15. Other conditions being equal, if one force is hurled against another ten times its size, the result will be the *flight* of the former.

16. When the common soldiers are too strong and their offi-cers too weak, the result is *insubordination*.

Tu Mu cites the unhappy case of T'ien Pu who was sent to Wei in A.D. 821 with orders to lead an army against Wang T'ing-ts'ou. But the whole time he was in command, his soldiers treated him with the utmost contempt, and openly flouted his authority by riding about the camp on donkeys, several thousands at a time. T'ien Pu was powerless to put a stop to this conduct, and when, after some months had passed, he made an attempt to engage the enemy, his troops turned tail and dispersed in every direction. After that, the unfortunate man committed suicide by cutting his throat.

When the officers are too strong and the common soldiers too weak, the result is *collapse*.

17. When the higher officers are angry and insubordinate, and on meeting the enemy give battle on their own account from a feeling of resentment, before the commander-in-chief can tell whether or no he is in a position to fight, the result is *ruin*.

18. When the general is weak and without authority; when his orders are not clear and distinct; when there are no fixed duties assigned to officers and men, and the ranks are formed in a slovenly haphazard manner, the result is utter *disorganisation*.

19. When a general, unable to estimate the enemy's strength, allows an inferior force to engage a larger one, or hurls a weak detachment against a powerful one, and neglects to place picked soldiers in the front rank, the result must be a *rout*.

20. These are six ways of courting defeat:

(1) 'neglect to estimate the enemy's strength', (2) 'want of authority'; (3) 'defective training'; (4) 'unjustifiable anger'; (5) 'non-observance of discipline'; (6) 'failure to use picked men'.

which must be carefully noted by the general who has attained a responsible post.

21. The natural formation of the country is the soldier's best ally; but a power of estimating the adversary, of controlling the forces of victory, and of shrewdly calculating difficulties, dangers and distances, constitutes the test of a great general.

22. He who knows these things, and in fighting puts his knowledge into practice, will win his battles. He who knows them not, nor practises them, will surely be defeated.

23. If fighting is sure to result in victory, then you must fight, even though the ruler forbid it; if fighting will not result in victory, then you must not fight even at the ruler's bidding.

> 'The responsibility of setting an army in motion must devolve on the general alone; if advance and retreat are controlled from the Palace, brilliant results will hardly be achieved. Hence the god-like ruler and the enlightened monarch are content to play a humble part in furthering their country's cause [*lit.*, kneel down to push the chariot wheel].'

24. The general who advances without coveting fame and retreats without fearing disgrace,

> Wellington said that the hardest thing of all for a soldier is to retreat.

whose only thought is to protect his country and do good service for his sovereign, is the jewel of the kingdom.

25. Regard your soldiers as your children, and they will follow you into the deepest valleys; look on them as your own beloved sons, and they will stand by you even unto death.

> Tu Mu draws an engaging picture of the famous general Wu Ch'i, 'He wore the same clothes and ate the same food as the meanest of his soldiers, refused to have either a horse

to ride or a mat to sleep on, carried his own surplus rations wrapped in a parcel, and shared every hardship with his men. One of his soldiers was suffering from an abscess, and Wu Ch'i himself sucked out the virus. The soldier's mother, hearing this, began wailing and lamenting. Somebody asked her, saying: "Why do you cry? Your son is only a common soldier, and yet the commander-in-chief himself has sucked the poison from his sore." The woman replied. "Many years ago, Lord Wu performed a similar service for my husband, who never left him afterwards, and finally met his death at the hands of the enemy. And now that he has done the same for my son, he too will fall fighting I know not where."'

26. If, however, you are indulgent, but unable to make your authority felt; kind-hearted, but unable to enforce your commands; and incapable, moreover, of quelling disorder: then your soldiers must be likened to spoilt children; they are useless for any practical purpose.

Tu Mu recalls an instance of stern military discipline which occurred in A.D. 219, when Lü Mêng was occupying the town of Chiang-ling. He had given stringent orders to his army not to molest the inhabitants nor take anything from them by force. Nevertheless, a certain officer serving under his banner, who happened to be a fellow-townsman, ventured to appropriate a bamboo hat belonging to one of the people, in order to wear it over his regulation helmet as a protection against the rain. Lü Mêng considered that the fact of his being also a native of Ju-nan should not be allowed to palliate a clear breach of discipline, and accordingly he ordered his summary execution, the tears rolling down his face, however, as he did so. This act of severity filled the army with wholesome awe, and from that time forth even articles dropped in the highway were not picked up.

27. If we know that our own men are in a condition to attack,

but are unaware that the enemy is not open to attack, we have gone only halfway towards victory.

28. If we know that the enemy is open to attack, but are unaware that our own men are not in a condition to attack, we have gone only halfway towards victory.

29. If we know that the enemy is open to attack, and also know that our men are in a condition to attack, but are unaware that the nature of the ground makes fighting impracticable, we have still gone only halfway towards victory.

30. Hence the experienced soldier, once in motion, is never bewildered; once he has broken camp, he is never at a loss.

31. Hence the saying: If you know the enemy and know yourself, your victory will not stand in doubt; if you know Heaven and know Earth, you may make your victory complete.

XI The Nine Situations

1. Sun Tzǔ said: The art of war recognises nine varieties of ground: (1) Dispersive ground; (2) facile ground; (3) contentious ground; (4) open ground; (5) ground of intersecting highways; (6) serious ground; (7) difficult ground; (8) hemmed-in ground; (9) desperate ground.

2. When a chieftain is fighting in his own territory, it is dispersive ground.

> So called because the soldiers, being near to their homes and anxious to see their wives and children, are likely to seize the opportunity afforded by a battle and scatter in every direction. 'In their advance they will lack the valour of desperation, and when they retreat, they will find harbours of refuge.'

3. When he has penetrated into hostile territory, but to no great distance, it is facile ground.

4. Ground the possession of which imports great advantage to either side, is contentious ground.

> When Lü Kuang was returning from his triumphant expedition to Turkestan in A.D. 385, and had got as far as I-ho, laden with spoils, Liang Hsi, administrator of Liang-chou, taking advantage of the death of Fu Chien, King of Ch'in, plotted against him and was for barring his way into the province. Yang Han, governor of Kao-ch'ang, counselled him, saying: 'Lü Kuang is fresh from his victories in the west, and his soldiers are vigorous and mettlesome. If we oppose him in the shifting sands of the desert, we shall be no match for

him, and we must therefore try a different plan. Let us hasten
to occupy the defile at the mouth of the Kao-wu pass, thus
cutting him off from supplies of water, and when his troops
are prostrated with thirst, we can dictate our own terms
without moving. Or if you think that the pass I mention is too
far off, we could make a stand against him at the I-wu pass,
which is nearer. The cunning and resource of Tzŭ-fang himself
would be expended in vain against the enormous strength of
these two positions.' Liang Hsi, refusing to act on this advice,
was overwhelmed and swept away by the invader.

5. Ground on which each side has liberty of movement is open
ground.

6. Ground which forms the key to three contiguous states, so
that he who occupies it first has most of the Empire at his
command, is ground of intersecting highways.

7. When an army has penetrated into the heart of a hostile
country, leaving a number of fortified cities in its rear, it is
serious ground.

8. Mountain forests, rugged steeps, marshes and fens – all
country that is hard to traverse: this is difficult ground.

9. Ground which is reached through narrow gorges, and from
which we can only retire by tortuous paths, so that a small
number of the enemy would suffice to crush a large body of
our men: this is hemmed-in ground.

10. Ground on which we can only be saved from destruction
by fighting without delay, is desperate ground.

'Suppose an army invading hostile territory without the aid
of local guides: it falls into a fatal snare and is at the
enemy's mercy. A ravine on the left, a mountain on the
right, a pathway so perilous that the horses have to be
roped together and the chariots carried in slings, no

passage open in front, retreat cut off behind, no choice but to proceed in single file. Then, before there is time to range our soldiers in order of battle, the enemy in overwhelming strength suddenly appears on the scene. Advancing, we can nowhere take a breathing-space; retreating, we have no haven of refuge. We seek a pitched battle, but in vain; yet standing on the defensive, none of us has a moment's respite. If we simply maintain our ground, whole days and months will crawl by; the moment we make a move, we have to sustain the enemy's attacks on front and rear. The country is wild, destitute of water and plants; the army is lacking in the necessaries of life, the horses are jaded and the men worn-out, all the resources of strength and skill unavailing, the pass so narrow that a single man defending it can check the onset of ten thousand; all means of offence in the hands of the enemy, all points of vantage already forfeited by ourselves: in this terrible plight, even though we had the most valiant soldiers and the keenest of weapons, how could they be employed with the slightest effect?'

11. On dispersive ground, therefore, fight not. On facile ground, halt not. On contentious ground, attack not.

But rather let all your energies be bent on occupying the advantageous position first. 'The rule with regard to contentious ground is that those in possession have the advantage over the other side. If a position of this kind is secured first by the enemy, beware of attacking him. Lure him away by pretending to flee – to show your banners and sound your drums – make a dash for other places that he cannot afford to lose – trail brushwood and raise a dust – confound his ears and eyes – detach a body of your best troops, and place it secretly in ambuscade. Then your opponent will sally forth to the rescue.'

12. On open ground, do not try to block the enemy's way. On ground of intersecting highways, join hands with your allies.

13. On serious ground, gather in plunder.

'When an army penetrates far into the enemy's country, care must be taken not to alienate the people by injust treatment. Follow the example of the Han Emperor Kao Tsu, whose march into Ch'in territory was marked by no violation of women or looting of valuables. [*Nota bene:* this was in 207 B.C., and may well cause us to blush for the Christian armies that entered Peking in A.D. 1900. Thus he won the hearts of all.

In difficult ground, keep steadily on the march.

14. On hemmed-in ground, resort to stratagem.

'Try the effect of some unusual artifice'; and Tu Yu amplifies this by saying: 'In such a position, some scheme must be devised which will suit the circumstances, and if we can succeed in deluding the enemy, the peril may be escaped.' This is exactly what happened on the famous occasion when Hannibal was hemmed in among the mountains on the road to Casilinum, and to all appearances entrapped by the Dictator Fabius. The stratagem which Hannibal devised to baffle his foes was remarkably like that which T'ien Tan had also employed with success exactly 62 years before. When night came on, bundles of twigs were fastened to the horns of some 2000 oxen and set on fire, the terrified animals being then quickly driven along the mountain side towards the passes which were beset by the enemy. The strange spectacle of these rapidly moving lights so alarmed and discomfited the Romans that they withdrew from their position, and Hannibal's army passed safely through the defile.

On desperate ground, fight.

15. Those who were called skilful leaders of old knew how to

drive a wedge between the enemy's front and rear; to prevent co-operation between his large and small divisions; to hinder the good troops from rescuing the bad, the officers from rallying their men.

16. When the enemy's men were scattered, they prevented them from concentrating; even when their forces were united, they managed to keep them in disorder.

17. When it was to their advantage, they made a forward move; when otherwise, they stopped still.

'Having succeeded in thus dislocating the enemy, they would push forward in order to secure any advantage to be gained; if there was no advantage to be gained, they would remain where they were.'

18. If asked how to cope with a great host of the enemy in orderly array and on the point of marching to the attack, I should say: 'Begin by seizing something which your opponent holds dear; then he will be amenable to your will.'

19. Rapidity is the essence of war. Take advantage of the enemy's unreadiness, make your way by unexpected routes, and attack unguarded spots.

In A.D. 227, Mêng Ta, governor of Hsin-ch'êng under the Wei Emperor Wên Ti, was meditating defection to the House of Shu, and had entered into correspondence with Chu-ko Liang, Prime Minister of that State. The Wei general Ssŭ-ma I was then military governor of Wan, and getting wind of Mêng Ta's treachery, he at once set off with an army to anticipate his revolt, having previously cajoled him by a specious message of friendly import. Ssŭ-ma's officers came to him and said: 'If Mêng Ta has leagued himself with Wu and Shu, the matter should be thoroughly investigated before we make a move.' Ssŭ-ma I replied: 'Mêng Ta is an unprincipled man, and we ought to go and punish him at once, while he is still wavering and before he has thrown off the mask.' Then, by a series of forced marches, he brought his army under the walls of Hsin-ch'êng within the space of eight days. Now Mêng Ta had previously said in a letter to Chu-ko Liang: 'Wan is 1200 *li* from here. When the news of my revolt reaches Ssŭ-ma I, he will at once inform his Imperial Master, but it will be a whole month before any steps can be taken, and by that time my city will be well fortified. Besides, Ssŭ-ma I is sure not to come himself, and the generals that will be sent against us are not worth troubling about.' The next letter, however, was filled with consternation: 'Though only eight days have passed since I threw off my allegiance, an army is already at the city-gates. What miraculous rapidity is this!' A fortnight later, Hsin-ch'êng had fallen and Mêng Ta had lost his head. In A.D. 621, Li Ching was sent from K'uei-chou in Ssŭ-ch'uan to reduce the successful rebel Hsiao Hsien, who had set up as Emperor at the modern Ching-chou Fu in Hupeh. It was autumn, and the Yangtsze being then in flood, Hsiao Hsien never dreamt that his adversary would venture to come down through the gorges, and consequently made no preparations. But Li Ching embarked his army without loss of time, and was just about to start when the other generals implored him to postpone his departure until the river was in a less dangerous state for navigation. Li Ching replied: 'To the soldier, overwhelming speed is of paramount importance, and he must never miss opportunities. Now is the time to strike, before Hsiao Hsien even knows that we have got an army together. If we seize the present moment when the river is in flood, we shall appear before his capital with startling suddenness, like the thunder which is heard before you have time to stop your ears against it. This is the great principle in war. Even if he gets to know of our approach, he will have to levy his soldiers in such a hurry that they will not be fit to oppose us. Thus the full fruits of victory will be ours.' All came about as he predicted, and Hsiao Hsien was obliged to surrender, nobly stipulating that his people should be spared and he alone suffer the penalty of death.

20. The following are the principles to be observed by an invading force: The further you penetrate into a country, the greater will be the solidarity of your troops, and thus the defenders will not prevail against you.

21. Make forays in fertile country in order to supply your army with food.

22. Carefully study the well-being of your men, and do not overtax them. Concentrate your energy and hoard your strength.

Ch'ên recalls the line of action adopted in 224 B.C. by the famous general Wang Chien, whose military genius largely contributed to the success of the First Emperor. He had invaded the Ch'u State, where a universal levy was made to oppose him. But, being doubtful of the temper of his troops, he declined all invitations to fight and remained strictly on the defensive. In vain did the Ch'u general try to force a battle: day after day Wang Chien kept inside his walls and would not come out, but devoted his whole time and energy to winning the affection and confidence of his men. He took care that they should be well fed, sharing his own meals with them, provided facilities for bathing, and employed every method of judicious indulgence to weld them into a loyal and homogeneous body. After some time had elapsed, he told off certain persons to find out how the men were amusing themselves. The answer was, that they were contending with one another in putting the weight and long-jumping. When Wang Chien heard that they were engaged in these athletic pursuits, he knew that their spirits had been strung up to the required pitch and that they were now ready for fighting. By this time the Ch'u army, after repeating their challenge again and again, had marched away eastwards in disgust.

The Ch'in general immediately broke up his camp and followed them, and in the battle that ensued they were routed with great slaughter. Shortly afterwards, the whole of Ch'u was conquered by Ch'in.

Keep your army continually on the move, and devise unfathomable plans.

23. Throw your soldiers into positions whence there is no escape, and they will prefer death to flight. If they will face death, there is nothing they may not achieve. Officers and men alike will put forth their uttermost strength.

24. Soldiers when in desperate straits lose the sense of fear. If there is no place of refuge, they will stand firm. If they are in the heart of a hostile country, they will show a stubborn front. If there is no help for it, they will fight hard.

25. Thus, without waiting to be marshalled, the soldiers will be constantly on the *qui vive*; without waiting to be asked, they will do your will; without restrictions, they will be faithful; without giving orders, they can be trusted.

26. Prohibit the taking of omens, and do away with superstitious doubts. Then, until death itself comes, no calamity need be feared.

'Spells and incantations should be strictly forbidden, and no officer allowed to inquire by divination into the fortunes of an army, for fear the soldiers' minds should be seriously perturbed. The meaning is that if all doubts and scruples are discarded, your men will never falter in their resolution until they die.'

27. If our soldiers are not overburdened with money, it is not because they have a distaste for riches; if their lives are not unduly long, it is not because they are disinclined to longevity.

'Wealth and long life are things for which all men have a

natural inclination. Hence, if they burn or fling away valuables, and sacrifice their own lives, it is not that they dislike them, but simply that they have no choice.' Soldiers are but human, it is for the general to see that temptations to shirk fighting and grow rich are not thrown in their way.

28. On the day they are ordered out to battle, your soldiers may weep, those sitting up bedewing their garments, and those lying down letting the tears run down their cheeks.

> Not because they are afraid, but because, as Ts'ao Kung says, 'all have embraced the firm resolution to do or die.'

But let them once be brought to bay, and they will display the courage of a Chu or a Kuei.

> Chuan Chu, a native of the Wu State and contemporary with Sun Tzǔ himself, who was employed by Kung-tzǔ Kuang, better known as Ho Lü Wang, to assassinate his sovereign Wang Liao with a dagger which he secreted in the belly of a fish served up at a banquet. He succeeded in his attempt, but was immediately hacked to pieces by the king's bodyguard. This was in 515 B.C. The other hero referred to, Ts'ao Kuei, performed the exploit which had made his name famous 166 years earlier in 681 B.C. Lu had been thrice defeated by Ch'i, and was just about to conclude a treaty surrendering a large slice of territory, when Ts'ao Kuei suddenly seized Huan Kung, the Duke of Ch'i, as he stood on the altar steps and held a dagger against his chest. None of the Duke's retainers dared to move a muscle, and Ts'ao Kuei proceeded to demand full restitution, declaring that Lu was being unjustly treated because she was a smaller and weaker state. Huan Kung, in peril of his life, was obliged to consent, whereupon Ts'ao Kuei flung away his dagger and quietly resumed his place amid the terrified assemblage without having so much as changed colour. As was to be expected, the Duke wanted afterwards to repudiate the

bargain, but his wise old counsellor Kuan Chung pointed out to him the impolicy of breaking his word, and the upshot was that this bold stroke regained for Lu the whole of what she had lost in three pitched battles.

29. The skilful tactician may be likened to the *shuai-jan*. Now the *shuai-jan* is a snake that is found in the Ch'ang mountains. Strike at its head, and you will be attacked by its tail; strike at its tail, and you will be attacked by its head; strike at its middle, and you will be attacked by head and tail both.

30. Asked if an army can be made to imitate the *shuai-jan*, I should answer, Yes. For the men of Wu and the men of Yüeh are enemies; yet if they are crossing a river in the same boat and are caught by a storm, they will come to each other's assistance just as the left hand helps the right.

The meaning is: If two enemies will help each other in a time of common peril, how much more should two parts of the same army, bound together as they are by every tie of interest and fellow-feeling. Yet it is notorious that many a campaign has been ruined through lack of co-operation, especially in the case of allied armies.

31. Hence it is not enough to put one's trust in the tethering of horses, and the burying of chariot wheels in the ground.

It is not enough, says Sun Tzŭ, to render flight impossible by such mechanical means. You will not succeed unless your men have tenacity and unity of purpose, and, above all, a spirit of sympathetic co-operation. This is the lesson which can be learned from the *shuai-jan*.

32. The principle on which to manage an army is to set up one standard of courage which all must reach.

Wellington's seemingly ungrateful description of his army at Waterloo as 'the worst he had ever commanded' meant no more than that it was deficient in this important particular – unity of spirit and courage. Had he not foreseen the Belgian defections and carefully kept those troops in the background, he would almost certainly have lost the day.

33. How to make the best of both strong and weak – that is a question involving the proper use of ground.

'The way to eliminate the differences of strong and weak and to make both serviceable is to utilise accidental features of the ground.' Less reliable troops, if posted in strong positions, will hold out as long as better troops on more exposed terrain. The advantage of position neutralises the inferiority in stamina and courage.

34. Thus the skilful general conducts his army just as though he were leading a single man, willy-nilly, by the hand.

35. It is the business of a general to be quiet and thus ensure secrecy; upright and just, and thus maintain order.

36. He must be able to mystify his officers and men by false reports and appearances, and thus keep them in total ignorance.

In the year A.D. 88 'Pan Ch'ao took the field with 25,000 men from Khotan and other Central Asian states with the object of crushing Yarkand. The King of Kutcha replied by dispatching his chief commander to succour the place with an army drawn from the kingdoms of Wên-su, Ku-mo and Wei-t'ou, totalling 50,000 men. Pan Ch'ao summoned his officers and also the King of Khotan to a council of war, and said: "Our forces are now outnumbered and unable to make head against the enemy. The best plan, then, is for us to separate and disperse, each in a different direction. The King of Khotan will march away by the easterly route, and I will then return myself towards the west. Let us wait until the evening drum has sounded and then start.' Pan Ch'ao now secretly released the prisoners whom he had taken alive, and the King of Kutcha was thus informed of his plans. Much elated by the news, the latter set off at once at the head of 10,000 horsemen to bar Pan Ch'ao's retreat in the west, while the King of Wên-su rode eastwards with 8000 horse in order to intercept the King of Khotan. As soon as Pan Ch'ao knew that the two chieftains had gone, he called his divisions together, got them well in hand, and at cock-crow hurled them against the army of Yarkand, as it lay encamped. The barbarians, panic-stricken, fled in confusion, and were closely pursued by Pan Ch'ao. Over 5000 heads were brought back as trophies, besides immense spoils in the shape of horses and cattle and valuables of every description. Yarkand then capitulating, Kutcha and the other kingdoms drew off their respective forces. From that time forward, Pan Ch'ao's prestige completely overawed the countries of the west.'

37. By altering his arrangements and changing his plans, he keeps the enemy without definite knowledge. By shifting his camp and taking circuitous routes, he prevents the enemy from anticipating his purpose.

38. At the critical moment, the leader of an army acts like one who has climbed up a height and then kicks away the ladder behind him. He carries his men deep into hostile territory before he shows his hand.

39. He burns his boats and breaks his cooking-pots; like a shepherd driving a flock of sheep, he drives his men this way and that, and none knows whither he is going.

40. To muster his host and bring it into danger – this may be termed the business of the general.

Sun Tzŭ means that after mobilisation there should be no delay in aiming a blow at the enemy's heart. Among the warring states of ancient China, desertion was no doubt a much more present fear and serious evil than it is in the armies of to-day.

41. The different measures suited to the nine varieties of ground; the expediency of aggressive or defensive tactics; and the fundamental laws of human nature: these are things that must most certainly be studied.

'One must not be hide-bound in interpreting the rules for the nine varieties of ground.'

42. When invading hostile territory, the general principle is, that penetrating deeply brings cohesion; penetrating but a short way means dispersion.

43. When you leave your own country behind, and take your army across neighbouring territory, you find yourself on critical ground. When there are means of communication on all four sides, the ground is one of intersecting highways.

44. When you penetrate deeply into a country, it is serious ground. When you penetrate but a little way, it is facile ground.

45. When you have the enemy's strongholds on your rear, and narrow passes in front, it is hemmed-in ground. When there is no place of refuge at all, it is desperate ground.

46. Therefore, on dispersive ground, I would inspire my men with unity of purpose. On facile ground, I would see that there is close connection between all parts of my army.

47. On contentious ground, I would hurry up my rear.

'If there is a favourable position lying in front of you, detach a picked body of troops to occupy it; then if the enemy, relying on their numbers, come up to make a fight for it, *you may fall quickly on their rear* with your main body, and victory will be assured.'

48. On open ground, I would keep a vigilant eye on my defences.

As Wang Hsi says, 'fearing a surprise attack.'

On ground of intersecting highways, I would consolidate my alliances.

49. On serious ground, I would try to ensure a continuous stream of supplies. On difficult ground, I would keep pushing on along the road.

50. On hemmed-in ground, I would block any way of retreat to make it seem that I mean to defend the position, whereas my real intention is to burst suddenly through the enemy's lines.

In A.D. 532, Kao Huan, afterwards Emperor and canonised as Shên-wu, was surrounded by a great army under Êhr-chu Chao and others. His own force was comparatively small, consisting only of 2000 horse and something under 30,000 foot. The lines of investment had not been drawn very closely together, gaps being left at certain points. But Kao Huan, instead of trying to escape, actually made a shift to block all the remaining outlets himself by driving into them a number of oxen and donkeys roped together. As soon as his officers and men saw that there was nothing for it but to conquer or die, their spirits rose to an extraordinary pitch of exalta-tion, and they charged with such desperate ferocity that the opposing ranks broke and crumbled under their onslaught.

On desperate ground, I would proclaim to my soldiers the hope-lessness of saving their lives.

'Burn your baggage and impedimenta, throw away your stores and provisions, choke up the wells, destroy your cooking-stoves, and make it plain to your men that they cannot survive, but must fight to the death.' Mei Yao-ch'ên says epigrammatically: 'The only chance of life lies in giving up all hope of it.'

51. For it is the soldier's disposition to offer an obstinate resistance when surrounded, to fight hard when he cannot help himself, and to obey promptly when he has fallen into danger.

'In A.D. 73 when Pan Ch'ao arrived at Shan-shan, Kuang, the King of the country, received him at first with great politeness and respect, but shortly afterwards his behaviour underwent a sudden change, and he became remiss and negligent. Pan Ch'ao spoke about this to the officers of his suite: "Have you not noticed," he said, "that Kuang's polite intentions are on the wane? This must signify that envoys have come from the Northern barbarians, and that consequently he is in a state of indecision, not knowing with which side to throw in his lot. That surely is the reason. The truly wise man, we are told, can perceive things before they have come to pass; how much more, then, those that are already manifest!" Thereupon he called one of the natives who had been assigned to his service, and set a trap for him, saying: "Where are those envoys from the Hsiung-nu who arrived some days ago?" The man was so taken aback that between surprise and fear he presently blurted out the whole truth. Pan Ch'ao, keeping his informant carefully under lock and key, then summoned a general gathering of his officers, thirty-six in all, and began drinking with them. When the wine had mounted into their heads a little, he tried to rouse their spirit still further by addressing them thus: "Gentlemen, here we are in the heart of an isolated region, anxious to achieve riches and honour by some great exploit. Now it happens that an ambassador from the Hsiung-nu arrived in this kingdom only a few days ago, and the result is that the respectful courtesy extended towards us by our royal host has disappeared. Should this envoy prevail upon him to seize our party and hand us over to the Hsiung-nu, our bones will become food for the wolves of the desert. What are we to do?" With one accord, the officers replied: "*Standing as we do in peril of*

84

our lives, we will follow our commander through life and death.'''

52. We cannot enter into alliance with neighbouring princes until we are acquainted with their designs. We are not fit to lead an army on the march unless we are familiar with the face of the country – its mountains and forests, its pitfalls and precipices, its marshes and swamps. We shall be unable to turn natural advantages to account unless we make use of local guides.

53. To be ignorant of any one of the following four or five principles does not befit a warlike prince.

54. When a warlike prince attacks a powerful state, his generalship shows itself in preventing the concentration of the enemy's forces. He overawes his opponents, and their allies are prevented from joining against him.

> Mei Yao-ch'ên constructs one of the chains of reasoning that are so much affected by the Chinese: 'In attacking a powerful state, if you can divide her forces, you will have a superiority in strength; if you have a superiority in strength, you will overawe the enemy; if you overawe the enemy, the neighbouring states will be frightened; and if the neighbouring states are frightened, the enemy's allies will be prevented from joining her.'

55. Hence he does not strive to ally himself with all and sundry, nor does he foster the power of other states. He carries out his own secret designs, keeping his antagonists in awe. Thus he is able to capture their cities and overthrow their kingdoms.

56. Bestow rewards without regard to rule, issue orders without regard to previous arrangements; and you will be able to handle a whole army as though you had to do with but a single man.

> 'In order to prevent treachery your arrangements should not

be divulged beforehand. There should be no fixity in your rules and arrangements.' Not only is there danger in letting your plans be known, but war often necessitates the entire reversal of them at the last moment.

57. Confront your soldiers with the deed itself, never let them know your design. When the outlook is bright, bring it before their eyes, but tell them nothing when the situation is gloomy.

58. Place your army in deadly peril, and it will survive; plunge it into desperate straits, and it will come off in safety.

These words of Sun Tzŭ were once quoted by Han Hsin in explanation of the tactics he employed in one of his most brilliant battles. In 204 B.C., he was sent against the army of Chao, and halted ten miles from the mouth of the Ching-hsing pass, where the enemy had mustered in full force. Here, at midnight, he detached a body of 2000 light cavalry, every man of which was furnished with a red flag. Their instructions were to make their way through narrow defiles and keep a secret watch on the enemy. 'When the men of Chao see me in full flight,' Han Hsin said, 'they will abandon their fortifications and give chase. This must be the sign for you to rush in, pluck down the Chao standards and set up the red banners of Han in their stead.' Turning then to his other officers, he remarked: 'Our adversary holds a strong position, and is not likely to come out and attack us until he sees the standard and drums of the commander-in-chief, for fear I should turn back and escape through the mountains.' So saying, he first of all sent out a division consisting of 10,000 men, and ordered them to form in line of battle with their backs to the River Ti. Seeing this manæuvre, the whole army of Chao broke into loud laughter. By this time it was broad daylight, and Han Hsin, displaying the generalissimo's flag, marched out of the pass with drums beating, and was immediately engaged by the enemy. A great battle followed, lasting for some time; until at length Han Hsin and his colleague Chang Ni, leaving drums and banner on the field, fled to the division on the river bank, where another fierce battle was raging. The enemy rushed out to pursue them and to secure the trophies, thus denuding their ramparts of men; but the two generals succeeded in joining the other army, which was fighting with the utmost desperation. The time had now come for the 2000 horsemen to play their part. As soon as they saw the men of Chao following up their advantage, they galloped behind the deserted walls, tore up the enemy's flags and replaced them by those of Han. When the Chao army turned back from the pursuit, the sight of these red flags struck them with terror. Convinced that the Hans had got in and overpowered their king, they broke up in wild disorder, every effort of their leader to stay the panic being in vain. Then the Han army fell on them from both sides and completed the rout, killing a great number and capturing the rest, amongst whom was King Ya himself . . . After the battle, some of Han Hsin's officers came to him and said: 'In the *Art of War* we are told to have a hill or tumulus on the right rear, and a river or marsh on the left front. You, on the contrary, ordered us to draw up our troops with the river at our back. Under these conditions, how did you manage to gain the victory?' The general replied: 'I fear you gentlemen have not studied the *Art of War* with sufficient care. Is it not written there: '*Plunge your army into desperate straits and it will come off in safety; place it in deadly peril and it will survive*'? Had I taken the usual course, I should never have been able to bring my colleagues round. If I had not placed my troops in a position where they were obliged to fight for their lives, but had allowed each man to follow his own discretion, there would have been a general *débandade*, and it would have been impossible to do anything with them.' The officers admitted the force of his argument, and said: 'These are higher tactics than we should have been capable of.'

59. For it is precisely when a force has fallen into harm's way that it is capable of striking a blow for victory.

Danger has a bracing effect.

60. Success in warfare is gained by carefully accommodating ourselves to the enemy's purpose.

'Feign stupidity' – by an appearance of yielding and falling in with the enemy's wishes. Chang Yü's note makes the meaning clear: 'If the enemy shows an inclination to advance, lure him on to do so; if he is anxious to retreat, delay on purpose that he may carry out his intention.' The object is to make him remiss and contemptuous before we deliver our attack.

61. By persistently hanging on the enemy's flank, we shall succeed in the long run in killing the commander-in-chief.

Always a great point with the Chinese.

62. This is called ability to accomplish a thing by sheer cunning.

63. On the day that you take up your command, block the frontier passes, destroy the official tallies, and stop the passage of all emissaries.

Either to or from the enemy's country.

64. Be stern in the council-chamber, so that you may control the situation.

65. If the enemy leaves a door open, you must rush in.

66. Forestall your opponent by seizing what he holds dear, and subtly contrive to time his arrival on the ground.

67. Walk in the path defined by rule, and accommodate yourself to the enemy until you can fight a decisive battle.

'Discard hard and fast rules. Victory is the only thing that matters, and this cannot be achieved by adhering to conventional canons.'

68. At first, then, exhibit the coyness of a maiden, until the enemy gives you an opening; afterwards emulate the rapidity of a running hare, and it will be too late for the enemy to oppose you.

XII The Attack by Fire

1. Sun Tzǔ said: There are five ways of attacking with fire. The first is to burn soldiers in their camp; the second is to burn stores; the third is to burn baggage-trains; the fourth is to burn arsenals and magazines; the fifth is to hurl dropping fire amongst the enemy.

Pan Ch'ao, sent on a diplomatic mission to the King of Shan-shan, found himself placed in extreme peril by the unexpected arrival of an envoy from the Hsiung-nu [the mortal enemies of the Chinese]. In consultation with his officers, he exclaimed: 'Never venture, never win! Unless you enter the tiger's lair, you cannot get hold of the tiger's cubs. The only course open to us now is to make an assault by fire on the barbarians under cover of night, when they will not be able to discern our numbers. Profiting by their panic, we shall exterminate them completely; this will cool the King's courage and cover us with glory, besides ensuring the success of our mission.' The officers all replied that it would be necessary to discuss the matter first with the Intendant. Pan Ch'ao then fell into a passion: 'It is to-day,' he cried, 'that our fortunes must be decided! The Intendant is only a humdrum civilian, who on hearing of our project will certainly be afraid, and everything will be brought to light. An inglorious death is no worthy fate for valiant warriors.' All then agreed to do as he wished. Accordingly, as soon as night came on, he and his little band quickly made their way to the barbarian camp. A strong gale was blowing at the time. Pan Ch'ao ordered ten of the party to take drums and hide behind the enemy's barracks, it being arranged that when they saw flames shoot up, they should begin drumming and yelling with all their might. The rest of his men, armed with bows and crossbows, he posted in ambuscade at the gate of the camp. He then set fire to the place from the windward side, whereupon a deafening noise of drums and shouting arose on the front and rear of the Hsiung-nu, who rushed out pell-mell in frantic disorder. Pan Ch'ao slew three of them with his own hand, while his companions cut off the heads of the envoy and thirty of his suite. The remainder, more than a hundred in all, perished in the flames. On the following day, Pan Ch'ao went back and informed Kuo Hsün [the Intendant] of what he had done. The latter was greatly alarmed and turned pale. But Pan Ch'ao, divining his thoughts, said with uplifted hand: 'Although you did not go with us last night, I should not think, Sir, of taking sole credit for our exploit.' This satisfied Kuo Hsün, and Pan Ch'ao, having sent for Kuang, King of Shan-shan, showed him the head of the barbarian envoy. The whole kingdom was seized with fear and trembling, which Pan Ch'ao took steps to allay by issuing a public proclamation. Then, taking the king's son as hostage, he returned to make his report to Tou Ku.

2. In order to carry out an attack with fire, we must have means available; the material for raising fire should always be kept in readiness.

3. There is a proper season for making attacks with fire, and special days for starting a conflagration.

4. The proper season is when the weather is very dry; the special days are those when the moon is in the constellations of the Sieve, the Wall, the Wing or the Crossbar; for these four are all days of rising wind.

5. In attacking with fire, one should be prepared to meet five possible developments:

6. (1) When fire breaks out inside the enemy's camp, respond at once with an attack from without.

7. (2) If there is an outbreak of fire, but the enemy's soldiers remain quiet, bide your time and do not attack.

The prime object of attacking with fire is to throw the enemy into confusion. If this effect is not produced, it means that the enemy is ready to receive us. Hence the necessity for caution.

8. (3) When the force of the flames has reached its height, follow it up with an attack, if that is practicable; if not, stay where you are.

'If you see a possible way, advance; but if you find the difficulties too great, retire.'

9. (4) If it is possible to make an assault with fire from without, do not wait for it to break out within, but deliver your attack at a favourable moment.

'If the enemy is settled in a waste place littered with quantities of grass, or if he has pitched his camp in a position which can be burnt out, we must carry our fire against him at any seasonable opportunity, and not wait on in hopes of an outbreak occurring within, for fear our opponents should themselves burn up the surrounding vegetation, and thus render our own attempts fruitless.'

10. (5) When you start a fire, be to windward of it. Do not attack from the leeward.

'When you make a fire, the enemy will retreat away from it; if you oppose his retreat and attack him then, he will fight desperately, which will not conduce to your success.' A rather more obvious explanation is given by Tu Mu: 'If the wind is in the east, begin burning to the east of the enemy, and follow up the attack yourself from that side. If you start the fire on the east side, and then attack from the west, you will suffer in the same way as your enemy.'

11. A wind that rises in the daytime lasts long, but a night breeze soon falls.

'A violent wind does not last the space of a morning.'

12. In every army, the five developments connected with fire must be known, the movements of the stars calculated, and a watch kept for the proper days.

'We must make calculations as to the paths of the stars, and watch for the days on which wind will rise, before making our attack with fire.'

13. Hence those who use fire as an aid to the attack show intelligence; those who use water as an aid to the attack gain an accession of strength.

14. By means of water, an enemy may be intercepted, but not robbed of all his belongings.

Water can do useful service, but it lacks the terrible destructive power of fire. This is the reason why the former is dismissed in a couple of sentences, whereas the attack by fire is discussed in detail.

15. Unhappy is the fate of one who tries to win his battles and succeed in his attacks without cultivating the spirit of enterprise for the result is waste of time and general stagnation.

'Those who want to make sure of succeeding in their battles and assaults must seize the favourable moments when they come and not shrink on occasion from heroic measures: that is to say, they must resort to such means of attack as fire, water and the like. What they must not do, and what will prove fatal, is to sit still and simply hold on to the advantages they have got.'

16. Hence the saying: The enlightened ruler lays his plans well ahead; the good general cultivates his resources.

> 'The warlike prince controls his soldiers by his authority, knits them together by good faith, and by rewards makes them serviceable. If faith decays, there will be disruption; if rewards are deficient, commands will not be respected.'

17. Move not unless you see an advantage; use not your troops unless there is something to be gained; fight not unless the position is critical.

18. No ruler should put troops into the field merely to gratify his own spleen; no general should fight a battle simply out of pique.

19. If it is to your advantage, make a forward move; if not, stay where you are.

20. Anger may in time change to gladness; vexation may be succeeded by content.

21. But a kingdom that has once been destroyed can never come again into being; nor can the dead ever be brought back to life.

22. Hence the enlightened ruler is heedful, and the good general full of caution. This is the way to keep a country at peace and an army intact.

XIII The Use of Spies

1. Sun Tzŭ said: Raising a host of a hundred thousand men and marching them great distances entails heavy loss on the people and a drain on the resources of the State. The daily expenditure will amount to a thousand ounces of silver. There will be commotion at home and abroad, and men will drop down exhausted on the highways. As many as seven hundred thousand families will be impeded in their labour.

2. Hostile armies may face each other for years, striving for the victory which is decided in a single day. This being so, *to remain in ignorance of the enemy's condition simply because one grudges the outlay of a hundred ounces of silver in honours and emoluments, is the height of inhumanity.*

> Sun Tzŭ's argument is: unless you are kept informed of the enemy's condition, and are ready to strike at the right moment, a war may drag on for years. The only way to get this information is to employ spies, and *it is impossible to obtain trustworthy spies unless they are properly paid for their services.* But it is surely false economy to grudge a comparatively trifling amount for this purpose, when every day that the war lasts eats up an incalculably greater sum. This grievous burden falls on the shoulders of the poor, and hence Sun Tzŭ concludes that *to neglect the use of spies is nothing less than a crime against humanity.*

3. One who acts thus is no leader of men, no present help to his sovereign, no master of victory.

> This idea, that the true object of war is peace, has its root

in the national temperament of the Chinese. Even so far back as 597 B.C., these memorable words were uttered by Prince Chuang of the Ch'u State: 'The character for "prowess" is made up of "to stay" and "a spear" (cessation of hostilities). Military prowess is seen in the repression of cruelty, the calling in of weapons, the preservation of the appointment of Heaven, the firm establishment of merit, the bestowal of happiness on the people, putting harmony between the princes, the diffusion of wealth.'

4. Thus, what enables the wise sovereign and the good general to strike and conquer, and achieve things beyond the reach of ordinary men, is *foreknowledge*.

That is, knowledge of the enemy's dispositions, and what he means to do.

5. Now this foreknowledge cannot be elicited from spirits; it cannot be obtained inductively from experience, nor by any deductive calculation.

6. Knowledge of the enemy's dispositions can only be obtained from other men.

'Knowledge of the spirit-world is to be obtained by divination; information in natural science may be sought by inductive reasoning; the laws of the universe can be verified by mathematical calculation: but the dispositions of an enemy are ascertainable through spies and spies alone.'

7. Hence the use of spies, of whom there are five classes: (1) Local spies; (2) inward spies; (3) converted spies; (4) doomed spies; (5) surviving spies.

8. When these five kinds of spy are all at work, none can discover the secret system. This is called 'divine manipulation of the threads.' It is the sovereign's most precious faculty.

Cromwell, one of the greatest and most practical of all cavalry leaders, had officers styled 'scout masters,' whose business it was to collect all possible information regarding the enemy, through scouts and spies, etc., and much of his success in war was traceable to the previous knowledge of the enemy's moves thus gained.

9. Having *local spies* means employing the services of the inhabitants of a district.

'In the enemy's country, win people over by kind treatment, and use them as spies.'

10. Having *inward spies*, making use of officials of the enemy.

'Worthy men who have been degraded from office, criminals who have undergone punishment; also, favourite concubines who are greedy for gold, men who are aggrieved at being in subordinate positions, or who have been passed over in the distribution of posts, others who are anxious that their side should be defeated in order that they may have a chance of displaying their ability and talents, fickle turncoats who always want to have a foot in each boat. Officials of these several kinds,' Sun Tzŭ continues, 'should be secretly approached and bound to one's interests by means of rich presents. In this way you will be able to find out the state of affairs in the enemy's country, ascertain the plans that are being formed against you, and moreover disturb the harmony and create a breach between the sovereign and his ministers.'
The necessity for extreme caution, however, in dealing with 'inward spies,' appears from an historical incident related by Ho Shih: 'Lo Shang, Governor of I-chou, sent his general Wei Po to attack the rebel Li Hsiung of Shu in his stronghold at P'i. After each side had experienced a number of victories and defeats, the rebel leader Li Hsiung had recourse to the services of a certain P'o-t'ai, a native of Wu-tu. He began by having him whipped until the blood came, and then sent him off to Lo Shang, whom he was to delude by offering to

co-operate with him from inside the city, and to give a fire signal at the right moment for making a general assault. Lo Shang, believing these promises, marched out all his best troops, and placed Wei Po and others at their head with orders to attack at P'o-t'ai's bidding. Meanwhile, Li Hsiung's general, Li Hsiang, had prepared an ambuscade on their line of march; and P'o-t'ai, having reared long scaling-ladders against the city walls, now lighted the beacon-fire. Wei Po's men raced up on seeing the signal and began climbing the ladders as fast as they could, while others were drawn up by ropes lowered from above. More than a hundred of Lo Shang's soldiers entered the city in this way, every one of whom was forthwith beheaded. The rebel leader Li Hsiung then charged with all his forces, both inside and outside the city, and routed the enemy completely.'

11. Having *converted spies*, getting hold of the enemy's spies and using them for our own purposes.

By means of heavy bribes and liberal promises detaching them from the enemy's service, and inducing them to carry back false information as well as to spy in turn on their own countrymen.

12. Having *doomed spies*, doing certain things openly for purposes of deception, and allowing our own spies to know of them and report them to the enemy.

'We ostentatiously do things calculated to deceive our own spies, who must be led to believe that they have been unwittingly disclosed. Then, when these spies are captured in the enemy's lines, they will make an entirely false report, and the enemy will take measures accordingly, only to find that we do something quite different. The spies will thereupon be put to death.'

13. *Surviving spies*, finally, are those who bring back news from the enemy's camp.

This is the ordinary class of spies, properly so called, forming a regular part of the army. *'Your surviving spy must be a man of keen intellect, though in outward appearance a fool; of shabby exterior, but with a will of iron. He must be active, robust, endowed with physical strength and courage: thoroughly accustomed to all sorts of dirty work, able to endure hunger and cold, and to put up with shame and ignominy.'*

Ho Shih tells the following story of Ta-hsi Wu of the Sui dynasty: 'When he was governor of Eastern Ch'in, Shên-wu of Ch'i made a hostile movement upon Sha-yüan. The Emperor T'ai Tsu sent Ta-hsi Wu to spy upon the enemy. He was accompanied by two other men. All three were on horseback and wore the enemy's uniform. When it was dark, they dismounted a few hundred feet away from the enemy's camp and stealthily crept up to listen, until they succeeded in catching the passwords used by the army. Then they got on their horses again and boldly passed through the camp under the guise of night-watchmen; and more than once, happening to come across a soldier who was committing some breach of discipline, they actually stopped to give the culprit a sound cudgelling! Thus they managed to return with the fullest possible information about the enemy's dispositions, and received warm commendation from the Emperor, who in consequence of their report was able to inflict a severe defeat on his adversary.'

14. Hence it is that with none in the whole army are more intimate relations to be maintained than with spies. None should be more liberally rewarded. In no other business should greater secrecy be preserved.

That is to say, all communications with spies should be carried on 'mouth-to-ear'. Spies are attached to those who give them most, he who pays them ill is never served. They should never be known to anybody; nor should they know one another. When they propose anything very material, secure their persons, or have in your possession their wives and children as hostages for their fidelity. Never communicate anything to them but what it is absolutely necessary that they should know.

15. Spies cannot be usefully employed without a certain intuitive sagacity.

'In order to use them, one must know fact from falsehood, and be able to discriminate between honesty and double-dealing. Before using spies we must assure ourselves as to their integrity of character and the extent of their experience and skill. A brazen face and a crafty disposition are more dangerous than mountains or rivers; it takes a man of genius to penetrate such.'

16. They cannot be properly managed without benevolence and straightforwardness.

17. Without subtle ingenuity of mind, one cannot make certain of the truth of their reports.

'Be on your guard against the possibility of spies going over to the service of the enemy.'

18. Be subtle! be subtle! and use your spies for every kind of business.

19. If a secret pieces of news is divulged by a spy before the time is ripe, he must be put to death together with the man to whom the secret was told.

20. Whether the object to be crush an army, to storm a city, or to assassinate an individual, it is always necessary to begin by finding out the names of the attendants, the aides-de-camp, the door-keepers and sentries of the general in command. Our spies must be commissioned to ascertain these.

As the first step, no doubt, towards finding out if any of
these important functionaries can be won over by bribery.

21. The enemy's spies who have come to spy on us must be
sought out, tempted with bribes, led away and comfortably
housed. Thus they will become converted spies and available
for our service.

22. It is through the information brought by the converted
spy that we are able to acquire and employ local and inward
spies.

'We must tempt the converted spy into our service, because
it is he that knows which of the local inhabitants are greedy
of gain, and which of the officials are open to corruption.'

23. It is owing to his information, again, that we can cause the
doomed spy to carry false tidings to the enemy.

'Because the converted spy knows how the enemy can best
be deceived.'

24. Lastly, it is by his information that the surviving spy can be
used on appointed occasions.

25. The end and aim of spying in all its five varieties is knowledge of the enemy; and this knowledge can only be derived, in
the first instance, from the converted spy.

He not only brings information himself, but makes it possible
to use the other kinds of spy to advantage.

Hence it is essential that the converted spy be treated with the
utmost liberality.

26. Of old, the rise of the Yin dynasty was due to I Chich who
had served under the Hsia. Likewise, the rise of the Chou
dynasty was due to Lü Ya who had served under the Yin.

27. Hence it is only the enlightened ruler and the wise general

who will use the highest intelligence of the army for purposes of spying, and thereby they achieve great results.

> Tu Mu closes with a note of warning: 'Just as water, which carries a boat from bank to bank, may also be the means of sinking it, so reliance on spies, while productive of great results, is oft-times the cause of utter destruction.'

Spies are a most important element in war, because on them depends an army's ability to move.

> An army without spies is like a man without ears or eyes.

The art of war is of vital importance to the state.
It is a matter of life and death, a road either to safety or to ruin.
Hence, it is a subject of inquiry, which can on no account, be neglected by any one of us
today
... and tomorrow.